Australian Working Holiday Makers
for
100 thousand dollars

Bruce Yoon

DEDICATION

To all the adventurous souls who have taken the leap to explore Australia on a Working Holiday Visa, this book is dedicated to you. May the experiences you have and the memories you make last a lifetime. Your bravery, curiosity, and hard work are an inspiration to us all. May this guide serve as a helpful companion on your journey, and may your time in Australia be filled with wonder, growth, and joy.

CONTENTS

PROLOGUE 1

Chapter 1 Introduction to the System and Visa 3

    What is a Working Holiday (WH) visa? 4

    WH Visa Eligibility 7

    document preparation....................................... 10

    HOW TO APPLY FOR WH VISA........................ 12

    health examination... 15

    2nd and 3rd Working Holiday visas 19

Chapter 2 Preparation before departure 23

    Making Flight Reservations................................ 24

    packing 27

    Prohibited Items for Import 30

    violation of quarantine laws 32

    Traveler's Insurance and Mobile Phone 35

Chapter 3 What to Do After Arrival 37

    Emergency phone numbers in Australia................. 38

    FREE INTERPRETATION SERVICE 40

    Driving in Australia.. 42

    Purchasing a vehicle....................................... 44

The way to check a vehicle's security interest 49

Chapter 4: Wisdom of Life 51

Friction with a car dealer...52

When a traffic accident occurs 54

A Case of alcohol offence...57

Introduction to Car Accident Case.......................................61

rent a house 64

Preparing an English Resume 67

Applying for an Australian Tax File Number (TFN) 72

Chapter 5. Is Earning 100 Thousand Dollars within a year Possible? 78

Qualifications for Employment 79

Getting a job..81

The average wage in Australia 85

Is it possible to earn 100 THOUSAND dollars in a year? 87

Australian taxes and tax savings 90

What are some suitable jobs for working holiday makers?.....92

Annexure..95

1. Sample Working Holiday Visa Application 96

2. Letter to Car Dealer...106

3. Sample Resume 107

Australian Working Holiday Maker for 1 million dollars

ACKNOWLEDGMENTS

I would like to express my deepest gratitude to my family for their unwavering patience and support as I worked on this book. To my partner, thank you for understanding the countless hours I spent researching, writing, and editing. Your patience with my hectic schedule and long absences from family gatherings has been truly remarkable.

PROLOGUE

Australia is a popular destination for many travelers each year due to its stunning natural landscapes and diverse cultural attractions. Among them, the Working Holiday visa is a visa that allows people to work and gain various experiences while staying in Australia, making it a popular choice for those who want a unique experience in Australia.

The Australia Working Holiday visa is available for young people between the ages of 18 and 30 who want to work and gain various experiences in Australia for a year. It is possible to experience various cultures and grow oneself by experiencing different cultures and interacting with different people while working in Australia.

However, obtaining an Australian Working Holiday visa requires a lot of effort. Knowing various information from visa applications to living tips in Australia can make life in Australia easier.

This book covers everything about the Australia Working Holiday visa in detail and provides information about living in Australia. This book will be helpful to those interested in living in Australia and those who want to have a new experience in Australia.

In particular, this book provides information on the process of applying for an Australian Working Holiday visa, necessary documents, and ways to find work easily in Australia. Some Working Holiday visa holders claim to have earned one billion won (approximately one million dollars) during their stay in Australia. This book explores whether this claim is true and provides insight on how one could earn such a significant amount of money during a year-long stay.

Australia is a land of endless possibilities. Start your journey to experience new things in Australia today!

CHAPTER 1 INTRODUCTION TO THE SYSTEM AND VISA

WHAT IS A WORKING HOLIDAY (WH) VISA?

The Working Holiday Maker (WHM) program is a reciprocal agreement that allows young people from over 40 partner countries to experience Australian culture, lifestyle, and job opportunities. The program has been in place since 1975 and has played a significant role in promoting personal connections and cultural exchange between Australia and partner countries, with a particular focus on the youth.

The WHM program allows young people aged between 18 and 35 (inclusive) to take a 12-month holiday in Australia and engage in short-term work and study. The program's main objectives are to provide participants with an opportunity to experience Australian culture and way of life while supplementing their travel funds through short-term work.

The WHM program was first introduced in 1975 to promote tourism and cultural exchange between Australia and the United Kingdom (UK), Ireland, and Canada. The program was later expanded to include more partner countries, including Korea, and is now available to young people from over 40 countries worldwide.

Over the years, the program has undergone several changes to ensure efficiency and sustainability. For example, in 2005, the Australian government introduced the Working Holiday Maker visa, allowing program participants to stay in Australia for up to 12 months and work for one employer for up to six months.

In 2016, the Australian government made additional changes to the program, such as increasing the age limit from 30 to 35 for certain countries and expanding the number of places available to program participants. The government also reduced visa application fees and introduced a 15% tax for the Working Holiday Maker.

The Australian Working Holiday Maker program has played a vital role in promoting cultural exchange and personal connections between Australia and partner countries since its inception in 1975. As a program that allows young people to supplement their travel funds through short-term work and gain valuable experiences, it has undergone several changes over the years to ensure efficiency and sustainability. It remains a popular program among young people worldwide, particularly offering them with valuable experiences and opportunities. We hope that you too can achieve your dream of exploring Australia through this program.

There are two subclasses available for Australian Working Holiday Visa: Subclass 417 and Subclass 462.
- Subclass 417, also known as the Working Holiday Visa, is available to citizens of certain countries including the United States, Canada, United Kingdom, and some European countries. This visa allows individuals to work and travel in Australia for up to 12 months, with the option to extend for another 12 months under certain conditions.
- Subclass 462, also known as the Work and Holiday Visa, is available to citizens of certain countries including Argentina, Chile, Indonesia, Thailand, and Turkey, among others. This visa also allows individuals to work and travel in Australia for up to 12 months, with the option to extend for another 12 months under certain conditions.

While both visas share many similarities, such as age requirements and work restrictions, the primary difference is the list of eligible countries for each subclass. It is important for individuals to check their eligibility for each subclass before applying.

WH VISA ELIGIBILITY

The Australian Working Holiday Visa is available to young adults aged between 18 and 30 (inclusive) who do not have dependent children and are citizens of eligible countries. As of 2023, the visa is divided into three stages and allows for a three-year stay in Australia.

To be eligible for the first stage of the Working Holiday Visa, applicants must meet the following criteria:
- have not previously entered Australia on a Working Holiday Visa
- be between the ages of 18 and 30 (inclusive) at the time of application
- hold a valid passport from an eligible country
- have sufficient funds to support themselves while in Australia (approximately AUD 5,000)
- meet health and character requirements
- Pass a health examination
- Have no criminal record and meet the required personal character standards

Once granted the visa, recipients are free to work in Australia, but cannot work for the same employer for more than six months. Additionally, they may study for up to four months, and if they wish to continue studying, they must apply for a student visa. If applicants are planning to apply for the second stage of the visa, they must provide evidence of having worked in a designated industry for at least three months.

You might not be eligible for this visa if you have had a visa cancelled or refused while you were in Australia.

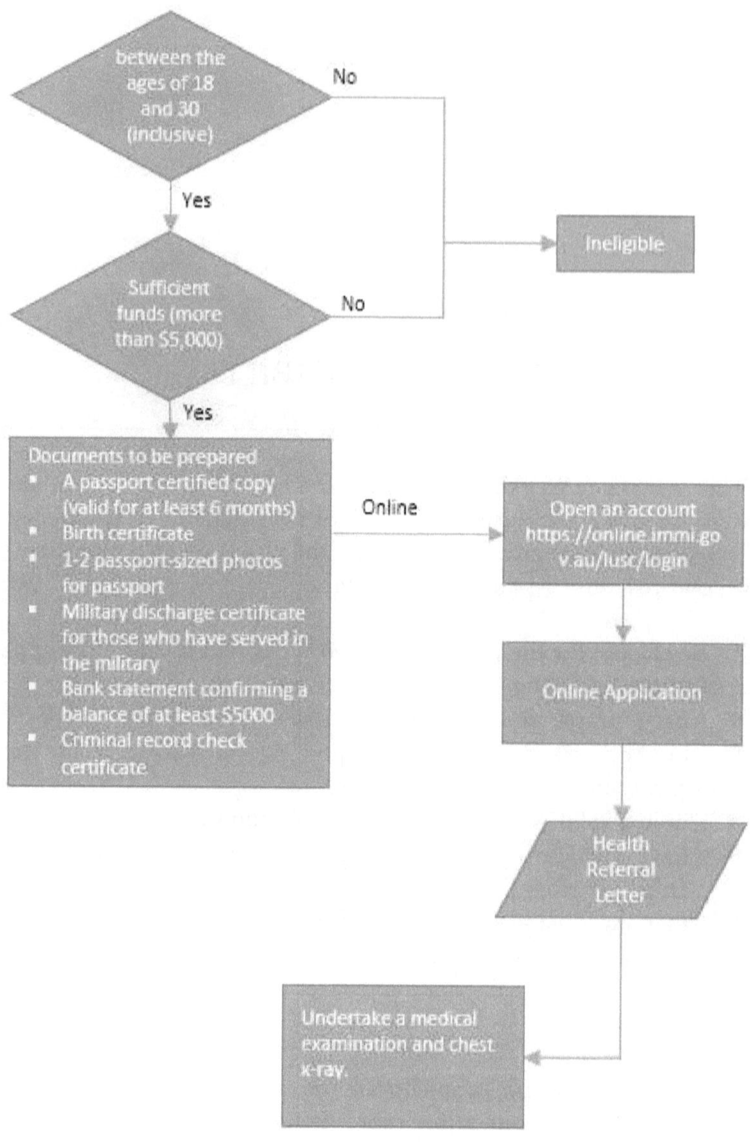

If you or any family members (including those who don't apply for the visa with you) owe the Australian government money, you or they must have paid it back or arranged to pay it back.

A quick tip about Australia!

In Australia, the standard voltage is 230-240 volts AC, and the frequency is 50 Hz. The electrical plugs and sockets used in Australia are Type I, which have two or three flat pins in a V-shape. The third pin is an earthing pin for safety purposes.

DOCUMENT PREPARATION

To apply for an Australian Working Holiday Visa (1st), you will need to prepare the following documents:

- Valid passport: You must have a valid passport issued by your country of citizenship.
- Online application: You will need to fill out an online application form and submit it along with the required documents.
- Passport-sized photos: You will need to provide two recent passport-sized photos.
- Proof of financial support: You will need to provide evidence of sufficient funds to support yourself during your stay in Australia. This can be in the form of a bank statement or letter, showing that you have at least AUD 5,000 in your account.
- Proof of health insurance: You will need to have health insurance for the duration of your stay in Australia.
- Character documents: You will need to provide police clearance certificates from all the countries you have lived in for 12 months or more in the last 10 years.
- Other documents: Depending on your circumstances, you may need to provide additional documents such as a resume, educational certificates, and proof of employment.

It is important to note that these requirements may change, so it is best to check the official Australian immigration website for the most up-to-date information.

If you are planning to apply for a second visa, it is necessary to provide evidence that you have worked in a designated industry for at least 3 months, so please keep this in mind.

As of May 2023, the application fee for the Australian working holiday visa is AUD $510. The fee is payable at the time of submitting the online application and can be paid using a credit or debit card. The accepted card types are Visa, MasterCard, American Express, Diners Club, and JCB. It is important to note that the application fee is non-refundable, even if the visa application is rejected.

HOW TO APPLY FOR WH VISA

After receiving the visa, one can freely enter and exit Australia for up to 12 months without applying for another visa. Some working holidaymakers may visit their country during their working holiday period and apply for a travel visa upon re-entry, but it is unnecessary.

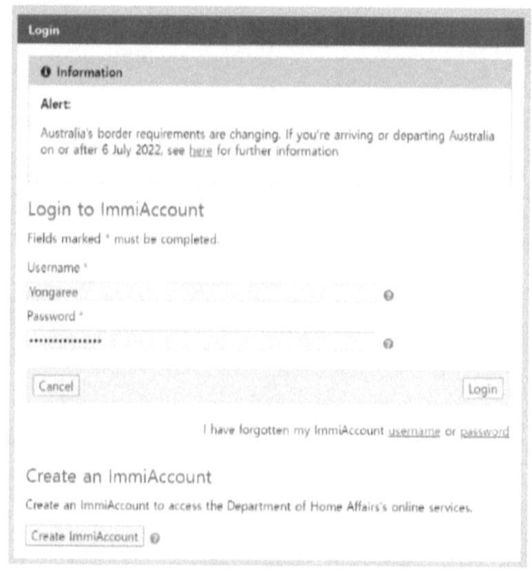

Figure 1-1

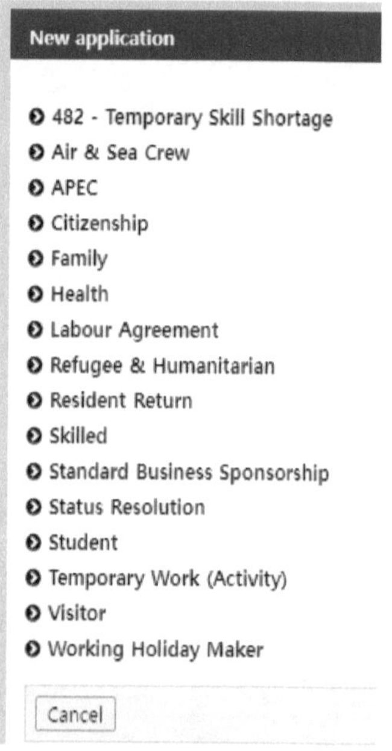

Figure 1-2

There are two ways to apply for a visa: through a migration agent or an immigration lawyer, or by applying oneself.
However, using a migration agent or lawyer incurs additional costs beyond the visa application fee, so one should consider their own abilities and

financial situation before deciding.

If you want to apply for a visa on your own, you must first go to the immigration department's website to create your account. To create an account, go to the immigration department's account creation page (https://online.immi.gov.au/lusc/login), enter your personal information, and register. Once you activate your account through your email, it will be available for immediate use (refer to Figure 1-1).

Once you have created your account, log in to your account and go to [My Application] -> [New Application] in the top left corner of the screen. You will see Figure 1-2.

Select [Working Holiday Maker] from the last menu. Two menus will appear, as shown in Figure 1-3.

○ Working Holiday Maker
Work and Holiday Visa (462)
Working Holiday Visa (417)

Figure 1-3

All people from the United States, Canada, United Kingdom, and some European countries including Japan and Republic of Korea must select [Working Holiday Visa (417)] and for people from Argentina, Chile, Indonesia, Thailand, and Turkey etc, select [Working Holiday Visa (462)]. The first screen that appears is shown in Figure 1-4. Simply enter your truthful answers to the questions on the screen and proceed by clicking [Next]. The actual application form is attached at the end of this booklet for reference.

Figure 1-4

Below are some selected questions that may be unfamiliar.

- Legal Status - If you hold citizenship of your country, select "Citizen".
- Will the applicant be accompanied by dependent children at any time during their stay in Australia on this visa? - The answer should be "No". If you answer "Yes", you will not be eligible to apply.
- Place of issue / issuing authority - fill in such as "Ministry of Foreign Affairs" as stated in their passport.
- Place of birth - Only the city or district of birth needs to be filled in. Detailed address of birthplace is not necessary. For example:

- Town / City: Dongrae-gu
- State / Province: Busan
- Country of birth: KOREA (SO STATED)
- Authorised recipient - Since you are applying directly, you should answer "No".
- For the questions in Health Declarations and Character Declarations, most of them should be answered "No". If you are a Korean male who has served in the military, you should answer "Yes" to the following question in Character Declarations and fill in your enlistment date, discharge date, rank at discharge, and details of military service:

Has any applicant ever served in a military force, police force, state sponsored/private militia or intelligence agency (including secret police)?

And for the Working Holiday Declarations **and** Declarations sections, all questions should be answered "Yes."

Once you have filled out the online form, you will be prompted to attach supporting documents on the final screen. Simply upload each prepared document to the system.

After entering the visa application information and paying the Australian $510 visa application fee (as of May 2023) online, the visa application process is complete.

A quick tip about Australia!

If you're planning a long-distance road trip outside the city, it's best to fill up your tank whenever you see a gas station. Australia is a vast country, and gas stations are often hundreds of kilometers apart from each other. It's common to run into trouble if you think you can make it to the next gas station with the gas you have left in your tank.

HEALTH EXAMINATION

The next step is to undergo a health examination. To do so, you need to first click on the "E-Medical Referral letter" option that appears after completing the online visa application and print it out. Fill in the required information and then go to a designated hospital in your country to receive the health examination.

In order to find the hospital in your country, you must click the link below in your internet browser.

https://immi.homeaffairs.gov.au/help-support/contact-us/offices-and-locations/list

Then you will see the screen for you to type in your country. For this example, Chile was typed in.

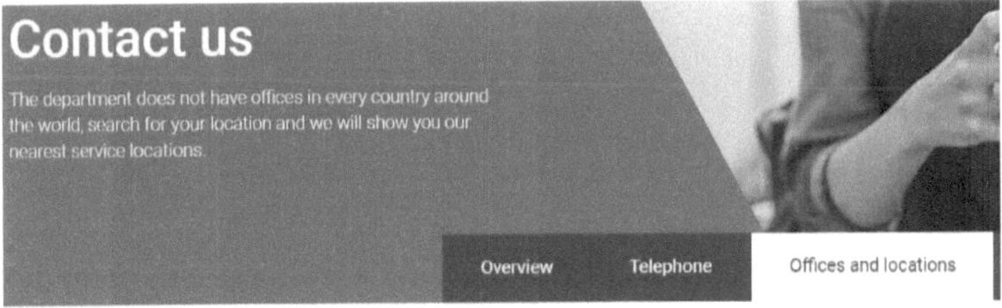

Then you will see the list of options as follows:-

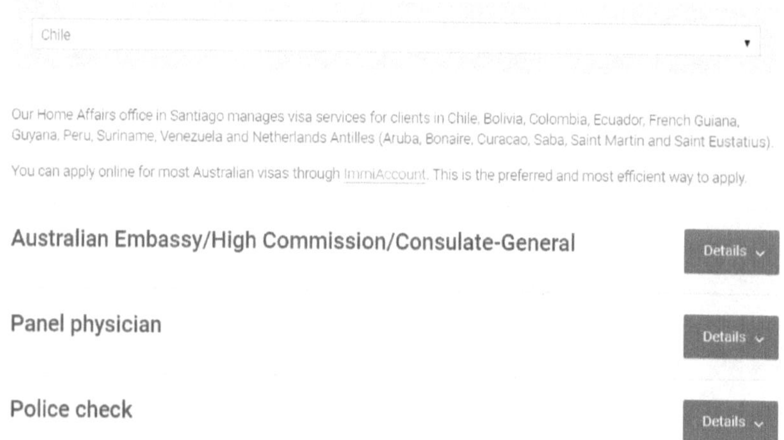

From here, you click "Details" of Panel physician and you will see contact details of the hospital which can perform your health examination.

You need to contact the hospital and arrange for your health examination.

The required documents for the health examination at the designated hospital include a passport, payment for the examination, one passport-sized photo, and the E-Medical Referral letter as shown in Figure 2-1 below. The examination typically takes about 1 to 1.5 hours.

Some precautions to keep in mind before the examination are that you should fast for at least 2 hours prior to the exam, females should avoid scheduling the exam during their menstrual cycle, and if your vision is less than 0.5, you should bring your glasses as corrected vision will be measured. If you have a history of lung disease, you should bring past chest X-ray films.

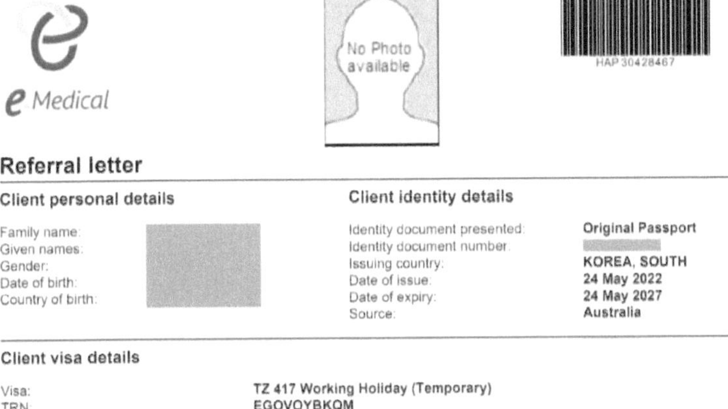

Referral letter

Client personal details		Client identity details	
Family name:		Identity document presented:	**Original Passport**
Given names:		Identity document number:	
Gender:		Issuing country:	**KOREA, SOUTH**
Date of birth:		Date of issue:	**24 May 2022**
Country of birth:		Date of expiry:	**24 May 2027**
		Source:	**Australia**

Client visa details

Visa:	**TZ 417 Working Holiday (Temporary)**
TRN:	**EGOVOYBKQM**
Visa Request ID:	**1885661280**

Figure 2-1

Australian Government

Department of Home Affairs

Dear

We have granted you a Working Holiday (subclass 417) visa on 05 January 2023.

Application status	
Working Holiday (subclass 417):	**Granted**

Visa conditions

8547 - Employer work limitation
8548 - Study limitation

An explanation of each condition of this Working Holiday (subclass 417) visa is included in this letter.

You can check these conditions at any time by using the Visa Entitlement Verification Online (VEVO) service. The four-digit number presented next to each condition above is used in VEVO to identify each condition that applies to this Working Holiday (subclass 417) visa.

Visa duration and travel

Date of grant	05 January 2023
For first entry, arrive by	05 January 2024

Figure 2-2

The health examination results will be sent to the Australian Embassy within 1-2 weeks. If there are no issues with your application documents or health examination results, you will receive your Working Holiday Visa within 1-2 weeks. The visa will be emailed to you as shown in Figure 2-2, and you should print it out and carry it with your passport when entering Australia. The visa must be used within 12 months from the issue date, or it will be cancelled.

2ND AND 3RD WORKING HOLIDAY VISAS

If you are experiencing Australia on a working holiday visa and thinking, "Wow, I like it here! I want to stay longer!" or "I need to make more money while I have the opportunity!" then you should prepare for a second or third working holiday visa.

If you have worked for more than 3 months in a specified work during your first working holiday visa, you may qualify for a second visa, and if you have worked for 6 months or more, you may qualify for a third visa. Since most of the jobs for these visas are in areas outside of Sydney, Melbourne, and Brisbane, it may be advantageous to establish yourself in areas with lower population density such as South or Western Australia, or Northern Territory from the beginning. However, if the sole purpose is to obtain a second or third working holiday visa qualification, it is recommended to confirm with the employer whether the job qualifies for the visa before starting work.

The following industries and areas are approved for specified work:
- tourism and hospitality in northern or remote and very remote Australia, from 22 June 2021
- plant and animal cultivation in regional Australia
- fishing and pearling in regional Australia
- tree farming and felling in regional Australia
- mining in regional Australia
- construction in regional Australia
- bushfire recovery work in declared bushfire affected areas only, after 31 July 2019
- flood recovery work in declared flood recovery areas only, undertaken on or after 1 January 2022, for applications lodged on or

- after 1 July 2022
- critical COVID-19 work in the healthcare and medical sectors anywhere in Australia, after 31 January 2020

Even if it is a job within the designated industry, please note that it will not be considered a specified work if it involves the following tasks:

Examples of ineligible specified work
- in tourism or hospitality:
  - ✓ cleaning work in a restaurant
  - ✓ driving a school bus
  - ✓ working as a sales assistant in a souvenir shop
- in Plant and animal cultivation:
  - ✓ working as a nanny on a farm
  - ✓ secondary processing or provision of plant and animal products, such as:
    - i. wine-making, brewing and distillation
    - ii. milling
    - iii. manufacturing of smallgoods
    - iv. retail of dairy or butchery products
    - v. giving wine tastings at a vineyard
- in mining:
  - ✓ performing specialised social science services (such as anthropological and archaeological assessments) for mining companies
  - ✓ cooking/catering on a mine site
  - ✓ cleaning the interior of mine complexes or buildings.
- in construction:
  - ✓ ship/boat building
  - ✓ manufacturing materials used on a construction site (such as concrete or steel)
  - ✓ town planning or architecture
- in bushfire recovery:
  - ✓ hospitality, cleaning or administrative work in a business that was not damaged by bushfire
  - ✓ construction or renovation work in an area that is not a declared bushfire affected area
  - ✓ work carried out on or before 31 July 2019
- in flood recovery:
  - ✓ hospitality, re-building, cleaning or administrative work in a business that was not damaged by floods
  - ✓ employment in a business not involved in flood recovery work

- ✓ clean-up, construction or any other work in an area that is not a declared flood affected area
  - ✓ work carried out on or before 31 December 2021
- in Critical COVID-19 work in the healthcare and medical sectors:
  - ✓ general administration or cleaning work with no connection to COVID-19
  - ✓ occupational therapy or physiotherapy for non-COVID-19 cases
  - ✓ financial and administrative services at a hospital, health or aged care facility
  - ✓ mental health support work not directly in response to COVID-19
  - ✓ work as a laboratory technician on vaccines other than for COVID-19
  - ✓ medical research other than for COVID-19
  - ✓ manufacturing or selling personal protective equipment or personal hygiene products

For eligible work within the designated industry, it must be done for at least 3 months for a send WH Visa or 6 months for a third WH Visa, but it is not necessary to work continuously for the required period. In other words, the cumulative period should be 3 months or 6 months, and if it is converted into days of work, it should be at least 88 days including weekends and holidays for 3 months and 179 days for 6 months.

Also, it is not necessary to work in the same occupation for the entire period. Therefore, if you work picking fruit on an orchard once and then herding sheep on a farm another time and the total working days add up to 88 days or 179 days, you are eligible to apply for a second or third WH Visa. Sometimes, if the number of days worked is miscalculated, the application for a second WH Visa may be rejected, so it is important to calculate carefully and make sure to ask the employer for a reference letter after finishing work.

You can apply for a second or third WH Visa within Australia or outside of Australia, just like when applying for the first visa. You can use the same online account with the immigration department that you opened when applying for your first visa to apply for the new visa.

A quick tip about Australia!
It is prohibited to drink alcohol in public places where alcohol is not permitted, without a liquor permit.

If you bring alcohol and drink it at a park or a scenic beach, thinking it feels good, you can be punished for violating liquor laws.

Chapter 2 Preparation before departure

MAKING FLIGHT RESERVATIONS

If you have obtained a working holiday visa, the next step is to book your flight. However, since flight prices can vary greatly, it is recommended to research and purchase tickets wisely. It is especially important to be aware of peak and off-peak seasons, as holidays in Australia and your country differ.

Skyscanner (https://www.skyscanner.co.kr/flights-to/au/cheap-flights-to-australia.html) is a popular travel search engine where you can search for flights from various cities in your country to different cities in Australia. As of February 26, 2023, according to their website, the cheapest round-trip airfare from Korea to Australia is approximately AUD$650, and the cheapest city to travel to in Australia is Sydney. It is important to note that flight prices and availability may change, so it is important to check for the latest information before making a reservation.

Alternatively, it is convenient to visit each airline's website to search for airfares. You can search for your preferred airline's website, such as Korean Air, Qantas, Singapore Airlines, or Malaysia Airlines, and choose the flight fares that vary depending on the departure date.

Another way to prepare for your trip to Australia is to visit the official Australian tourism website (https://www.australia.com/ko-kr/facts-and-planning/getting-around.html) to learn basic information about each region of Australia, such as its characteristics and distance.

When purchasing an airline ticket, it is important to inquire about the weight and size of baggage allowed by each airline, as each airline has its own limitations. It is also necessary to consider the weight and size of the luggage that you will bring.

If you are looking for a low-cost airline, you can use airlines such as Air Asia or Dragon Air. However, if there is a problem with the connecting route, low-cost airlines do not offer any compensation, so personally, the author does not recommend it, although many people prefer it because of the low price.

For reference, I'd like to share my experience. Before the pandemic, I once booked a flight for my parents to visit Australia through Air Asia. From the perspective of my parents who live in Busan, Air Asia departing from Gimhae International Airport felt more convenient than other flights departing from Incheon International Airport, and I felt that the price was relatively cheaper compared to Cathay Pacific in Hong Kong. The route was from Busan, via Kuala Lumpur (with about 3 hours of layover), to Perth. To make it more comfortable for my parents, I chose seats in a more comfortable area and made sure they could bring about 20kg of luggage each. I also introduced Air Asia to my daughter who was planning to visit Korea, and she also booked her flight with Air Asia, paid for it, received a Confirmation Message, and I even sent the e-tickets to my parents.

However, a week before the departure, I received an email from AirAsia. They said that due to their circumstances, they had canceled the connecting flight from Kuala Lumpur to Perth because it was not economically feasible. Instead, they had made a reservation for a flight to Perth three days later and asked if we would accept the change. Since AirAsia did not have a phone reservation service, we had to inquire by email, and they said it would take five days to respond. My parents, who couldn't speak English, asked if the airline could provide accommodation and a guide during the three days they would be staying in Kuala Lumpur, but AirAsia replied that as a low-cost carrier, such connection services had to be borne by the individual. Although I had a lot to say about their irresponsible behavior, I couldn't risk my parents' travel plans being ruined, so I had no choice but to cancel all of AirAsia's tickets and quickly rebook my parents' tickets on Cathay Pacific for the same date, which turned out to be not much different in price from AirAsia.

Later, a week before my daughter's departure, she also received a unilateral notice from AirAsia that the flight from Kuala Lumpur to Seoul had been canceled. We could not trust AirAsia's flight schedule, so we also canceled all of my daughter's AirAsia tickets. And it took a whopping three months to receive a refund from AirAsia.

Because of these bitter experiences, my family has decided not to use low-cost airlines again. However, whether to choose a low-cost airline or a regular airline is up to the readers' choice.

A Quick Tip About Australia!

Although Australia may be known for its sparse mountains, if you venture into the shrublands that resemble hills, you'll be surprised to find many of the plants that Koreans love, such as ferns, growing abundantly. However, unlike in Korea, freely collecting wild herbs or plants in nature can result in violating environmental conservation laws in Australia, and lead to penalties. Therefore, let's refrain from collecting them.

PACKING

One of the most serious things to consider before departing for Australia is what to bring with you. I remember when I first set foot on Australian soil, I thought that since Australia is a warm country, I only packed summer clothes and put everything else in my cargo. I figured that I could just buy cheap local products if I needed anything else. However, despite receiving several blankets from the flight attendants, I was still shivering alone on the plane because the air conditioning was so cold. And when I arrived at Perth at 6 a.m., the morning temperature was so cold that my teeth were chattering. I even considered buying a warm jacket somewhere, but there was nowhere to buy clothes at the airport or outside at that time of the day. Therefore, the first thing you need to pack is appropriate clothing (including innerwear) and shoes that can adapt to the extreme temperature differences.

Next, what you need to prepare is sufficient funds depending on your purpose. If you want to enjoy various cultural activities and even take language courses during your trip to Australia, you will need to prepare additional funds in addition to your living and transportation expenses. However, most people who come to Australia for a working holiday will not just be interested in tourism, but will be in a hurry to find a job within a short period of time. Therefore, when considering your expenses, you should also consider the amount you will need if you are unable to find a job within your planned time frame. According to immigration law as of February 2023, a minimum of $5,000 is required, but this is only the minimum necessary expense and may not be enough for everyone. If you have to live on this money without finding a job, assuming the lowest possible quality of life and trying to save as much as possible, you may be able to survive for about 6 to 10 months. Therefore, you should consider this as a guide when estimating your expenses.

As a side note, as a traveler, if you are 18 years old or older, you are allowed to bring tobacco products with you into Australia.

You do not need a permit to bring in tobacco products to Australia as a traveller.

You are allowed to bring in duty-free - one unopen packet of up to 25 cigarettes or 25 grams of other tobacco products and one open packet of cigarettes.

If you bring in tobacco you must declare any tobacco you have with you above the duty free allowance, pay all relevant duty and taxes that apply on arrival into Australia.

A Quick Tip about Australia!

As of February 26, 2023, the price of a pack of cigarettes in Australia is at least $41 for 20 cigarettes based on the Malboro brand. Compared to the price in Korea, which is around $5AUD per pack, it is almost 9 times more expensive. This is the highest cigarette price among 107 countries worldwide. Quitting smoking during your stay in Australia is a shortcut to saving money.

Once you have prepared as mentioned above, you now need to gather various necessary documents. Some of the documents that come to mind are as follows:

- Passport
- Driver's license
- International driver's license
- English resume
- Letter of recommendation from a previous employer.

If you have prepared as described above, now you need to gather the necessary documents. Some of the essential items when looking for a job in Australia are an English resume and a referral from your former employer. Please refer to the separate section below for tips on preparing these documents.

Please note that the electricity in Australia is 240V 50Hz, which may differ from your country's standard. This means that if you bring electronic devices from your country without considering the difference in power and frequency, you risk damaging your valuable electronic devices. I once brought a new Samsung drum washing machine from Korea to Australia, paying for the shipping cost. Until then, I believed that the difference in power and frequency had little effect on electronic devices. The reason was that my old LG refrigerator from Korea was still running well after decades. However, this drum washing machine broke down after only a month of use. It was impossible to find parts for the Korean product in Australia, and the repair cost was almost equivalent to buying a new one, so I had to dispose of it as recycling waste.

According to an electrical expert, most electrical products can tolerate a difference of about 20 volts, but products that rely on frequency-dependent electronic circuits can be damaged if they are used with different power and frequency. However, small electronic devices such as mobile phones or computers mostly use portable adapters, so the power and frequency difference between Australia and your country is not significant.

PROHIBITED ITEMS FOR IMPORT

Australia is known for its strict customs inspections, which are in place to protect the country's unique ecosystem and agricultural industry from potential invasive species or diseases. Therefore, it is crucial to be aware of items that are not allowed to be imported when packing for Australia.

Food: When it comes to food, homemade food is strictly prohibited from importation into Australia. Only commercially processed or unopened packaged food is allowed to be brought into the country. Meat, poultry, and fish must be processed products and cannot be raw or fresh. Additionally, only sealed products that can be stored at room temperature and have a shelf life of at least 6 months, such as canned goods, are allowed. Certain seafood items, such as oysters, are prohibited from importation except for those originating from New Zealand. However, other seafood items such as mussels, abalone, sea urchins, sea cucumbers, crabs, and lobsters are allowed as long as they are clean and in good condition.

Animals: When it comes to animals, there are many that are prohibited from importation into Australia due to the potential risk of introducing diseases or causing ecological harm. Animals can only be imported through an Australian government-approved importer. Generally, birds, wild boars, exotic animals, and exotic plants are prohibited from importation.

Plants: Importing plants into Australia is strictly prohibited in order to protect the unique flora and fauna of the country. Specifically, importing wildflowers, seeds, fruits, bark, and shells is prohibited. Even in cases where importation is allowed, it must be done through an Australian government-approved importer.

If you plan to import items into Australia, you will be subject to customs inspection, and prohibited items will be confiscated. Therefore, it is important to be aware of the regulations and be careful when packing. Additionally, if you plan to import items, you must provide a receipt or certificate of origin to prove that the item is of Australian origin.

VIOLATION OF QUARANTINE LAWS

With a heart full of excitement, some visitors to Australia have found themselves facing charges for violating quarantine laws after failing to declare food items at the airport.

While some may have genuinely forgotten to list their food items on the arrival card, others have intentionally lied or withheld information. In most cases, if the food is discovered during customs inspection, the individual is simply given a warning or a fine, but in more extreme cases, the person may face prosecution and have to appear in court.

It is well known that Australia has strict rules regarding food imports, but not all visitors may be aware of these regulations. Recently, a person was caught attempting to bring Korean food items into Perth Airport, including sausages, rice cake soup, and kimchi for their younger sibling studying in Australia. Despite the language barrier and their children experiencing motion sickness on the flight, the person claimed she had no food items to declare when asked by customs officials.

According to her account, she misunderstood the question when asked if she had any food items, mistaking the word "food" for "fruit". She also had trouble understanding and completing the arrival card due to her limited English skills and her children's discomfort. However, during the subsequent customs inspection, the food items were discovered, and she was charged with violating quarantine laws.

In some cases, a misinterpretation or mistake can lead to serious consequences, especially when language and cultural barriers are present. This highlights the importance of clear communication and understanding of regulations for international travelers.

Anyway, the information conveyed through the interpreter was that the individual knew she had brought food but omitted this fact on her immigration declaration card. Later, when asked by a customs officer, the interpreter only conveyed the fact that the individual answered that she didn't have any food, without explaining why she had initially omitted this information. This suggests that the interpreter did not perform their duties properly.

In any case, the individual was prosecuted for violating Article 67 of *the Quarantine Act* and Article 234 of *the Customs Act*. Article 67 of the Quarantine Act is stated as follows:

(a) the person imports, introduces, or brings into any port or other place in Australia, the Cocos Islands or Christmas Island any thing; and (Cocos 섬*, Christmas*

.

.

Maximum penalty: Imprisonment for 10 years.

Furthermore, Article 234 of the Customs Act is stated as follows:

(1) A person shall not:
(d) do any of the following:
(i) intentionally make or cause to be made a statement to an officer, reckless as to the fact that the statement is false or misleading in a material particular;

.

.

. . .a penalty not exceeding 500 penalty units.

She was charged under both Article 67 of *the Quarantine Act* and Article 234 of *the Customs Act* and came to me around 11 pm the night before the trial. Violation of Article 234 of *the Customs Act* carries a maximum fine of $25,000, but Article 67 of *the Quarantine Act* carries a maximum sentence of 10 years in prison without a fine, so they were facing a serious charge.

Imagine visiting Australia with a joyful heart and then being sentenced to 10 years in prison. She even brought her young children with her, but instead of enjoying the sights, she had to shuttle back and forth between the courthouse and her lawyer's office, not even being able to relax at home. I did my best to help her avoid an imprisonment sentence and empathize with her feelings as parent.

Fortunately, the next day in court, we received a promise from the prosecutor that they would not seek an imprisonment sentence, and she was able to get away with a light fine. If you try to hide and bring in food continuously, you may end up in a situation where it is difficult to avoid an imprisonment sentence. Therefore, if you are traveling to Australia, it is essential to honestly declare any food you are bringing with you as a cautionary case.

TRAVELER'S INSURANCE AND MOBILE PHONE

I would like to offer some advice for people who are considering whether to purchase travel insurance before departing for Australia and whether their home country mobile phone can be used as is.

Travel Insurance

When preparing for travel insurance, it is important to consider the coverage and benefits. You should check if you can receive compensation for travel inconveniences such as flight cancellations, medical expenses, and lost baggage during the trip. This protection is also a wise way to prevent unexpected problems from incurring costs.

There are two ways to purchase travel insurance: you can purchase it in your home country before departure, or purchase it upon arrival in Australia. However, it is not recommended to purchase insurance upon arrival in Australia as the insurance premium is twice as expensive as it is in Asian countries and there is a Waiting Period before the insurance claim can be made.

If you purchase travel insurance before departing from your home country, you can receive protection for medical expenses, flight cancellations, and other unforeseen problems, thereby reducing the financial burden in case of unexpected events. Some insurance products also compensate for losses such as lost baggage, so it is necessary to check the insurance policy carefully.

Mobile Phone

You can use your home country mobile phone in Australia, but it depends on your phone and your home country's mobile network provider. If your phone is unlocked and supports the Australian mobile network frequencies, you can use it with an Australian SIM card. However, roaming charges can be expensive, so it may be more cost-effective to purchase an Australian SIM card or a prepaid phone plan when you arrive in Australia. It is best to check with your mobile network provider before traveling to Australia to see if they offer international roaming or other options for using your phone abroad.

These days, people generally use SNS like WhatsApp or KakaoTalk more often, so they hardly use MMS, the messaging function on regular phones. Therefore, there is no problem using your home country mobile phone in Australia.

If you buy a prepaid SIM card at a mart or convenience store, you can plug it into your phone and register it for immediate use.

Chapter 3 What to Do After Arrival

EMERGENCY PHONE NUMBERS IN AUSTRALIA

During your stay in Australia, unexpected emergencies may occur. If this happens, it's important to stay calm and have the following emergency phone numbers on hand to get the help you need.

000 - Australian Emergency Services

If you find yourself in a life-threatening situation or a situation where time is of the essence, simply dial 000. This includes situations where your life or someone else's life is in danger, there is a serious injury that requires urgent medical attention, or if you witness a serious incident or crime and need to report it. By calling this number, you can connect with emergency services such as the police, fire department, or ambulance, even if you don't speak English. There is no charge for this call, and you won't incur any additional fees, so don't hesitate to use it when you need it.

112 - Auxiliary Emergency Phone Number in Australia

In Australia, you can also use 112 as an emergency phone number, just like in any other country. When you dial this number, you will be automatically connected to 000. This is useful for those who are more familiar with 112 than 000, as it is an international standard emergency number. However, please note that unlike 000, this number only works on digital mobile phones. If you try to dial this number from a landline, it will not work, so be sure to keep that in mind.

106 - Text Emergency Relay Service

For those who have hearing or speech impairments and are in a life-threatening or property-threatening situation, they can directly contact the police, fire department, or ambulance by using TTY (also known as a teletypewriter or text phone) to dial 106. Please note that emergency services cannot be contacted using SMS (Short Message Service) on mobile phones.

106 - Text Emergency Relay Service

For those with hearing or speech impairments who are in danger of life or property, you can directly contact the police, fire department, or ambulance through TTY (also known as a teletypewriter or text telephone) by dialing 106. Note that you cannot use SMS (Short Message Service) on your mobile phone to contact emergency services.

106 Service Usage Guide

- Press the recipient's charge telephone number, 106.
- A message will appear asking if you want the police (PPP type), fire truck (FFF type), or ambulance (AAA type). Note that if you can speak and listen, you can simply say "Police," "Fire," or "Ambulance" to the relay operator.
- The relay operator waits without hanging up the call to make a call to the correct service and relay your conversation.
- You don't have to tell your location because TTY is connected to a fixed line, so the emergency service receives your location as soon as you make the call.
- A message will appear asking you to confirm your address.

FREE INTERPRETATION SERVICE

In addition to emergency services, another useful information to know is the free interpreting service operated by the Australian government, called TIS National. As all Australian government agencies are connected to this free interpreting service, if you have any business with them, such as with the Australian Taxation Office, you can confidently request and use the interpreting service. If you want more detailed information, you can visit https://www.tisnational.gov.au/ to find out.

On-demand Phone Interpretation

If you call 131 450, you can use the on-the-spot telephone interpreting service provided by the free interpreting service 24 hours a day, every day of the year.

Reservation Phone Interpreting Service

If you need to schedule a consultation or interview with an organization and they require a phone interpreting service to be reserved in advance, this service can be useful. If you plan to visit an Australian government office for business purposes, the organization will typically arrange for a reservation phone interpreting service, so you only need to request your language interpreting services.

On-site Interpretation Service

On-site interpretation service is a service in which an interpreter comes to the reserved interpretation location and provides interpretation services. On-site interpretation services are widely used by Australian institutions seeking to communicate with non-English-speaking customers.

Procedure for using the free interpreting service 131 450:

When you call the free interpreting service, a TIS National operator will answer the call in English and ask what language you want to interpret in. If you want to request Korean, for example, you can simply say "Korean," and the operator will put the call on hold to find an available Korean interpreter. Even if there is no hold music, do not hang up and wait for the interpreter to be found.

When a Korean interpreter is found, the operator will connect you to the interpreter and ask which organization you want to speak to through the interpreter. It's convenient to have the name, phone number, and customer or account number (if available) of the organization you want to speak to ready in advance.

The TIS National operators must maintain neutrality, so they cannot assist in finding contact information or making requests. The interpreters must also maintain neutrality during the interpreting process and cannot engage in private conversations. If a Korean interpreter cannot be found, the operator will ask you to call back later.

DRIVING IN AUSTRALIA

When you first arrive in Australia, with a heart filled with excitement to explore this beautiful country with its clear blue skies and stunning rivers, one of the first things you will notice is the issue with public transportation. If you don't have your own car, it can be difficult to move around freely. Even with public transportation such as trains and buses, the intervals between them are often long, and even short distances can take hours to travel. Therefore, the first tip I always give to people who are new to Australia is to learn about the driver's licence. Firstly, it is possible to use your home country driver's licence in Australia.

With your home country driver's licence

The good news is that in most states and territories of Australia, you can use your valid overseas licence to drive for as long as it remains current, without the need to obtain an Australian driver's licence.

1.   **Carry an International Driving Permit (IDP) with you**

This IDP can be issued in your home country prior to coming to Australia, and it is valid in all countries that are members of the United Nations Convention on Road Traffic. As Australia is a member of this convention since December 7, 1954, the IDP can be used in Australia as a substitute for an Australian driver's license. However, it is required to carry your home country driver's license with you as well.

2.   **Carry a certified translation of your driver's license**

If you are a sensible person, you will likely prepare an International Driving Permit before leaving your home country. However, there may be some people like the author who occasionally lose their minds and forget about the International Driving Permit. In this case, a useful method is to carry an English translation of your home country driver's license along with the license. If you wish to carry a translation of your home country driver's license, you must have it translated by a person who has a qualification of at least level 3 from the National Accreditation Authority for Translators and Interpreters (NAATI).

However, since there are not many translators with NAATI qualifications, license translation may not be easy. In such cases, your embassy or consulate can provide translation services for a fee.

3.   Applying for an Australian driver's licence

If your home country has been included in the "Recognised Countries for Licence Exchange" program and you are over 25 years of age and have not had your driver's licence cancelled in the 12 months prior to applying, you can exchange your licence for an Australian driver's licence without taking any theory or practical tests.

It could be illegal to drive with your home country driver's licence in Australia if:

a.   You have been in Australia for more than three months and you are driving in the Northern Territory. In this case, you are required to obtain a Northern Territory issued driver's licence or apply for an exemption.

b.   Your home country driver's licence is expired or invalid.

c.   Your home country driver's licence is not written in English, and you do not have an International Driving Permit or a certified translation of your licence.

d.   You have been issued an Australian driver's licence due to the recognition of your home country driver's licence, but your home country licence is subsequently cancelled or suspended. In this case, your Australian licence may also be cancelled or suspended.

PURCHASING A VEHICLE

Australia is a vast country with a small population, so public transportation is not as developed as it is in Korea or European countries. As a result, it can be very inconvenient to use public transportation to travel unless you are in major cities such as Sydney or Melbourne. Even if there is public transportation where you live, having a car is necessary if you want to move around freely in Australia because the routes and intervals are not as diverse and fast as they are in other countries like Japan or Korea.

Also, buying and selling used cars in Australia is not complicated and very easy. Therefore, if you own a car while staying in Australia and sell it before leaving Australia, you can often make money by selling it at a higher price than when you bought it due to fluctuations in the price of used cars.

So where and how do you buy a car? If you have enough money to buy a new car, you can choose a car that suits your personal taste without hesitation. However, if you need to buy a used car, it is more important to consider the performance of the car than your personal taste in terms of price.

The following is roughly how to purchase a used car in Australia:

- Through personal introductions
- Through local newspaper advertisements
- Through online advertisements
- Through a used car dealer

Before anything else, when buying a used car, it's important to set a budget and determine the type of car and body style that you want. This will help you compare prices more easily and make a purchasing decision with less difficulty, as the prices of used cars can vary greatly.

If you have found a suitable used car, it's important to get in touch with the owner and ask for the following information:

- How long have they owned the car?
- Why are they selling it?
- Has the car been involved in any accidents or suffered any damage?
- What is the current condition of the car?
- Will it pass a Roadworthy Certificate (RWC)?

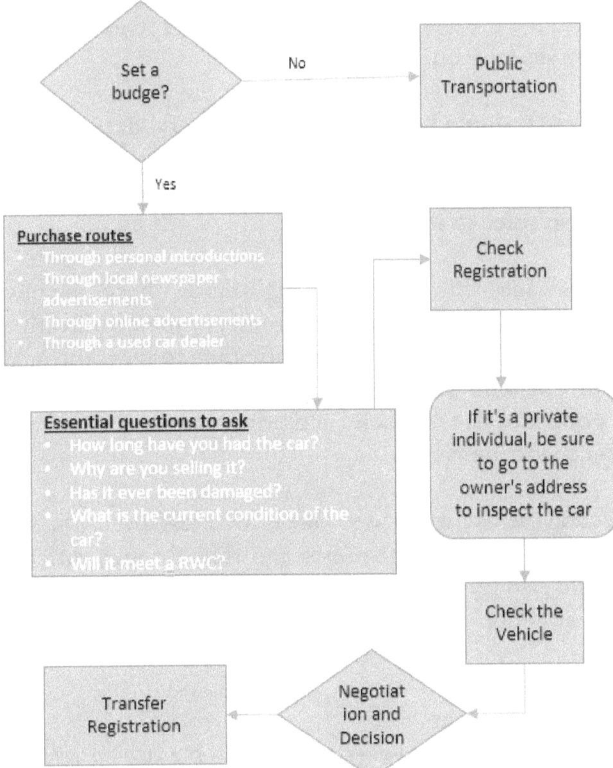

If the seller is a private individual rather than a used car dealer, it's important to print out the advertisement they posted and go to their address to inspect the car. This is necessary to verify whether the address on the registration certificate matches the seller's address. Additionally, you should bring the advertisement with you and verify that the condition of the car matches the description in the advertisement by referring to it and asking any relevant questions you may have.

If you're interested in the car, it's important to check if it's been stolen or if there are any liens on it by conducting a vehicle history check. Some states may charge a small fee for this service, but it's worth spending the money to avoid potential losses later on.

"Vehicle registration check" procedures vary depending on the state, so you should visit the website of the state you belong to and perform the check. Detailed instructions are provided in the next chapter, so please refer to it.

If there are no issues with the vehicle registration check, the next step is to inspect the car in person. You can arrange to see the car directly with the owner or dealer at their garage or set a specific time to meet them. While it's difficult for someone who isn't an expert to identify all the problems with a used car, it's a good idea to ask around and bring someone who knows about cars to help you check the vehicle.

After inspecting the car, it's time to take it for a test drive. During the test drive, listen for any strange engine noises and shift through different gears. Ideally, you should also try driving on various road conditions to identify any issues that need attention. Make a list of any problems you find during the test drive.

Tips for inspecting a car
- It is recommended to always inspect the car during daylight hours and avoid rainy or dark nights.
- Check for rust or welding marks on the car body, bonnet, and interior carpets.
- Check for oil leaks and verify that the oil level is appropriate under the bonnet.
- Thoroughly inspect the oil filter cap area for a white substance resembling mayonnaise, which may indicate a blown head gasket. Replacing this can be quite expensive.

- Check the tire treads for wear.
- Inspect the alignment of the front and rear wheels by looking straight down the car from the front wheel to the back wheel. If there is any deviation, it is a sign that the car has been in an accident.
- Inspect the gaps in the connecting points of the body panels. If the gaps are inconsistent, it is a sign that the car has been in an accident.
- Check the functionality of the seat belts and the proper movement of the seats. Inspect all the switches to ensure that they are functioning properly.
- Turn on the ignition when the engine is cold to verify that it starts without issue, and check that the exhaust is not emitting black smoke.

If you have decided to buy a car, it's okay to negotiate the price while explaining some potential issues to the car owner. You can ask the car owner directly,

"What is your best price?"

and if they give you a price, you can counter with a slightly lower offer.

Table of Internet Addresses of Driver's License Issuing Authorities	
State/Territory	**Internet Address**
New South Wales (NSW)	https://transportnsw.info/
Victoria (VIC)	https://www.ptv.vic.gov.au/
Queensland (QLD)	https://www.tmr.qld.gov.au/
South Australia (SA)	https://www.sa.gov.au/
Western Australia (WA)	https://www.transport.wa.gov.au/
Tasmania (TAS)	https://www.transport.tas.gov.au/
Australian Capital Territory (ACT)	https://www.transport.act.gov.au/
Northern Territory (NT)	https://nt.gov.au/driving

Once the price is confirmed, you can proceed to transfer ownership. The process of transferring ownership is not as difficult or complicated as in some other countries, and you can easily obtain a ownership transfer notification form from the driver's license agency or download it from the internet and send it by mail. You can refer to the internet address table of each footnote driver's license jurisdiction for the internet address to download the form.

THE WAY TO CHECK A VEHICLE'S SECURITY INTEREST

When purchasing a registered vehicle, it is important to check if the vehicle is under security interest. Even if the ownership of the vehicle has been transferred to one's name, if the vehicle has been offered as security, then the debt associated with it is also transferred. In Australia, checking for a vehicle's security interest is done through Personal Property Securities Register (PPSR), which is operated by the Australian Financial Security Authority. If a vehicle is found to have security interest, then it should not be bought.

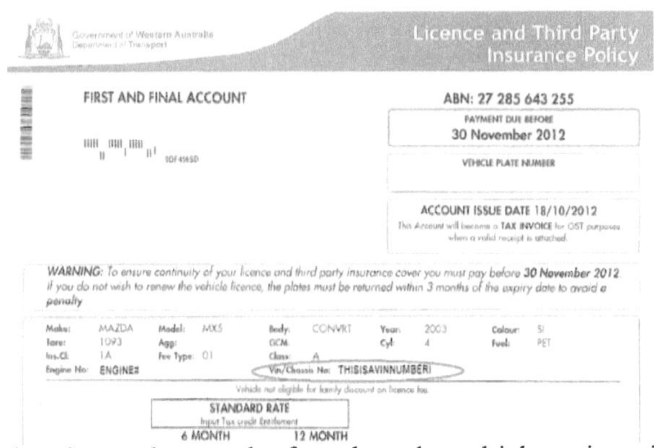

This kind of security interest check can be easily done by anyone online. All that is needed is the vehicle's VIN or chassis number and a payment of $2 for the search, which can be made using a credit card. The VIN or chassis number can be found on the vehicle registration certificate, as shown in the image on the left. The buyer can ask the seller to provide the VIN or chassis number as it appears on the certificate.

Furthermore, if you go to **https://www.ppsr.gov.au** on the internet, a

Figure 5-1

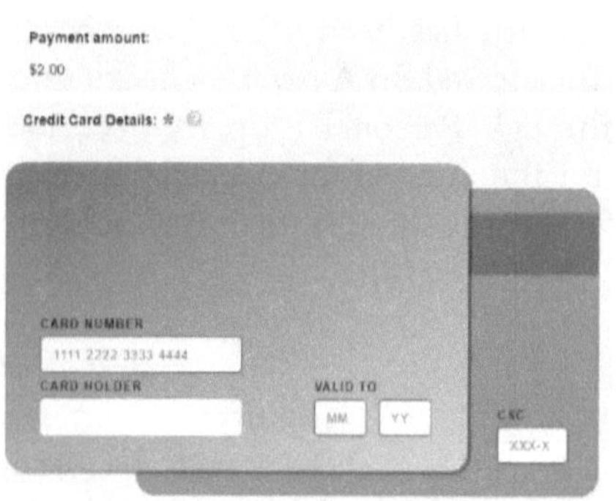

Figure 3-3

Figure 4-2

screen like Figure 3-1 appears.

Select [Do a $2 vehicle search] at the bottom right. Then, the [Quick motor vehicle search] screen appears, as shown in Figure 3-2, and you can press the [Continue] button at the bottom right or click the link that says [PPSR Car Check here] on the bottom left.

When the screen like Figure 3-3 appears, enter the VIN or Chassis number and enter your email address to receive the search result. Then, to pay the search fee of $2, enter your credit card information and press the [Pay Now] button, and the search is complete, and the vehicle search information will be sent to your email address.

Chapter 4: Wisdom of Life

FRICTION WITH A CAR DEALER

If you have purchased a car through a used car dealer and the car is causing problems contrary to the advertisement or dealer's description, what would you do? As a working holiday maker, purchasing a car in Australia would likely be the biggest expense, so if the car turned out to have significant defects contrary to expectations, handle it calmly as follows:

1.   Phone call explanation
First, explain the vehicle's defects to the responsible person over the phone and ask how they will resolve the issue.

2.   Written request
If the responsible person refuses the phone request or avoids answering, draft and send a written claim form.

3.   Report to the Consumer Protection Agency
If there is no response by the deadline even after sending the written claim form, report it to the Australian Competition and Consumer Commission (ACCC) with the written claim form. The contact information for the ACCC is as follows:
ACCC Domestic Reporting Phone: 1300 302 502
If calling from overseas: +61 2 6243 1305
Online Report Address https://www.accc.gov.au/contact-us/contact-the-accc/report-a-consumer-issue

A Quick Tip About Australia!
Used car dealers in Australia are required by law to sell cars of acceptable quality under the Consumer Protection Law. This means that the quality of the car must be one that an average person would expect, given the price, age,

and any descriptions provided at the time of sale. If you discover a major fault after purchasing the car, it can be considered as not of acceptable quality.

53

WHEN A TRAFFIC ACCIDENT OCCURS

When a traffic accident occurs in Australia, many people may feel confused and not know how to handle the situation, which can lead to further difficulties. If a car accident happens, it's important to remain calm and take the following steps:

Ensure Safety: Make sure that you and anyone else involved in the accident are safe. If possible, move your vehicle to a safe location and turn on your hazard lights to warn other drivers.

Call Emergency Services: If anyone is injured, call 000 immediately. Even if no one is injured, it's still important to contact the police to report the accident.

In addition to the above, you must acquire the following information.

Secure witnesses
The first priority is to secure witnesses. Ask if any drivers or pedestrians in the vicinity witnessed the accident and write down their names and contact information. If you are not fluent in English, quickly take action through someone who speaks English among your acquaintances in the area.

Information about the other vehicle
Write down the other driver's vehicle registration number and vehicle information (make, model, type, color, etc.). Also, sketch the accident scene and take photos of the vehicles before they are moved, if possible.

Information about the other driver
Ask the other driver for their driver's license and record their name,

address, and contact phone numbers. Some people may ask, "You're not a police officer, how can you ask for a driver's license?" but as parties involved in a traffic accident, they have the authority to verify each other's identity and can therefore ask for a driver's license. If the driver refuses to provide their license, contact the nearest police station or call "000" and report, "A driver without a license is involved in a traffic accident and is trying to flee." The police will immediately respond. Obtain this information through the police.

Other information

If there were passengers in the other car, obtain their personal information as well. Also, find out if the other driver is the owner of the car. If not, it is important to know who the actual owner is. Check if anyone was injured and record their personal information and the extent of their injuries.

Insurance-related

Ask the other driver if they have insurance and determine whether to process the claim through insurance or personally pay for damages.

1. If handling the repairs personally, go to a nearby auto repair shop together to get an estimate and request repair work. If the other driver is unable to provide the repair cost at the time, ask for a copy of the estimate to be sent to them by mail and request that they pay for it.

2. If processing through insurance, write down the name and phone number of the other driver's insurance company and request a claim number. Once you have the claim number, contact the insurance company and complete the claim form as required.

Police Report

If you want to report a traffic accident, you can go to the nearest police station or download a Crash Report from the internet and send it to the police station. You can easily report a traffic accident online without going to the police station. When reporting a traffic accident to the police, you need the following information:

- ✓ Date and time of the accident
- ✓ Accurate accident location
- ✓ Personal information such as driver's license number
- ✓ Vehicle-related information such as car registration number
- ✓ Personal information of the other driver, passengers, owner (if different from the driver), and witnesses
- ✓ Personal information of those injured in the accident
- ✓ Estimated amount of damage
- ✓ Accident details

If you are the at-fault driver, do not rush to say "I will take responsibility for everything" and seek assistance from your insurance company if you have insurance or quickly contact a nearby lawyer if you do not have insurance.

A CASE OF ALCOHOL OFFENCE

M, who came to Perth on a temporary visa, wandered around the night streets of Northbridge while drunk and received a police order to leave the streets near Northbridge from a patrolling police officer, citing an attempted theft of a wallet belonging to an aboriginal woman. Despite the order, M continued to linger in Northbridge and was arrested by the police for groping a white woman's chest from behind, leading to prosecution for violating police orders and committing sexual assault.

In countries following the common law legal system, such as Australia and the United States, the basic principle of criminal law is that an individual cannot be held criminally responsible unless they acted purposely or with recklessness. In Australia, this principle was upheld in a case that took place in 1980. The defendant, known as O, was a regular user of hallucinogens who stole a map from a car while under the influence of alcohol. When a police officer saw the theft and tried to arrest O, he drew a concealed knife and stabbed the officer. O was charged with assault with intent to cause bodily harm. However, because he was in a hallucinatory state, expert testimony showed that he was unable to make rational decisions and control his own will while under the influence of alcohol. Therefore, the case was sent back to a lower court based on the fundamental principle of criminal law that an individual cannot be held criminally liable for acts that were not committed intentionally or recklessly.

In 1997, a rugby player living in Canberra was charged with assaulting two women at a bar while he was drunk. However, he was later acquitted when it was confirmed that he was so intoxicated that the film of the incident was cut off. Following a series of alcohol-related incidents like this, Australian society became embroiled in a heated debate. The controversy centered around the conflict between the principle that only acts committed intentionally or recklessly can be subject to criminal liability, and the societal expectation that the law should protect society from criminals who drink alcohol freely and punish them.

As a result, in Queensland, Western Australia, Tasmania, and other states, criminal laws have been **codified** to deviate from the principle of common law in order to process cases related to alcohol according to the criminal code.

In the Western Australia Criminal Code Act section 28, it is stipulated that if a person suffers a mental or physical impairment due to addiction or anaesthesia, the defence of insanity may be considered. In contrast, while section 172 of the Tasmanian Criminal Code Act specifies that anyone who unlawfully harms or injures another person is punishable, section 13(1) of the same code states that there is no criminal liability unless the act is intentional or reckless.

Anyway, despite being unable to understand the English instructions given by the police while he was drunk, Mr. M was charged with disobeying police orders and sexual assault, which was difficult for him to comprehend even when he was sober. The next day, he woke up to find himself in a police cell.

Before meeting his friend, Mr. M had already been drunk after drinking a considerable amount of beer and soju. Together with two other friends, they drank nine bottles of soju within an hour, causing Mr. M to black out. He searched for people who could testify to what had happened, but all his friends who were with him at that time were also intoxicated and unable to provide any clear evidence to prove that he was incapable of consent due to being heavily intoxicated.

If convicted as charged, M could have faced imprisonment of 2-5 years and a maximum fine of $24,000. However, the most severe punishment would have been his inclusion in the sex offender list, which could have led to significant personal repercussions and international notoriety.

Although M initially resigned himself to a guilty plea in his impatience to put the case behind him, he eventually decided to fight the charges with the advice of the author, who urged him to avoid being listed as a sex offender at all costs.

First, because of M's English proficiency and intoxicated state, it was possible to refute the charge of disobeying police orders, for which the arrest warrant was issued, so M explained the situation to the police officer who issued the warrant and they agreed to withdraw the charge.

The problem was the charge of sexual assault, and the investigating police officer claimed that being drunk is not a legal defense. Furthermore, the prosecution insisted that even if M was drunk, they were confident in their guilty verdict and strongly refuted the defense's arguments. The prosecution's argument is not entirely wrong because committing a crime while under the influence of alcohol does not necessarily excuse the crime. However, if the illegal act was committed due to a state of mind that was completely unrelated to one's own will, like that of a person suffering from a sleepwalking disorder, the situation can be different. Nevertheless, it was not easy to prove that M was in such a state.

Since there were no witnesses in M's case, there were many difficulties. However, based on M's statement that he was in the police station detention center, M requested CCTV footage taken at the detention center and obtained testimony from friends and their wives who were drinking together at the time. Based on this evidence, M claimed that his actions were not deliberate or intentional, and as a result of pressuring the prosecution, M was ultimately acquitted.

When involved in a crime that one did not intend, it is important to have the wisdom to calmly reconsider the situation and respond appropriately.

INTRODUCTION TO CAR ACCIDENT CASE

I want to share with you a very interesting case that came before the High Court of Australia in April 2011. Through this case, I believe we can gain a significant understanding of Australia's legal principles. On May 17, 1998, a 16-year-old girl named Miller had been drinking late at night and found herself stranded without money to catch a bus or train home. As a result, she stole a car. However, she had neither a driver's license nor was in a fit state to drive due to alcohol consumption, so she asked her 27-year-old cousin Maurin Miller to drive for her.

Maurin, in his excitement, drove the car and as he picked up speed, Miller yelled, "Stop, let me out!" But Maurin ignored Miller's request and continued driving until he caused a major traffic accident. As a result of the accident, Miller suffered a permanent disability, and her family sued Maurin for damages.

The main issue in this lawsuit was whether Maurin had a duty of care to Miller.

First, in the District Court of Western Australia, Maurin found that Miller had a duty of care towards her, but on appeal, the court found that Miller and Maurin were accomplices in the car theft, so Maurin had no duty of care towards Miller as an accomplice, and overturned the decision of the district court.

The family then appealed to the High Court of Australia. On April 7, 2011, the High Court ruled by a majority decision that since Miller had withdrawn from the joint criminal enterprise of illegal use of the car just before the accident, Maurin had a duty of care to Miller. The Court held that Maurin did not owe a duty of care to Miller before the accident, as there was no continuing joint criminal enterprise at the time. In other words, when Miller shouted "stop, let me out!" just before the accident, she withdrew from the joint criminal enterprise and became a passenger in Maurin's car. Maurin violated his duty of care as a driver and caused the accident, which resulted in injury to Miller as his passenger.

WA News | News | Australia

Quadriplegic car thief can sue for crash

KATHERINE FLEMING | The West Australian
Fri, 8 April 2011 7:42AM

The case was sent back to the Western Australian District Court, and Miller's lawyers had agreed earlier that if it was decided that Morin had a duty of care, Miller would accept 50% responsibility for his injuries, so it is curious what kind of agreement the parties reached.

I recall a case from a few years ago where a group of 3-4 Korean workers rented a car together. They were unable to rent the car themselves due to various circumstances, so they rented it using the driver's license and credit card of another Australian citizen. While driving, an accident occurred and the driver and passengers suffered serious injuries. Those who rented the car under someone else's name were considered accomplices for the crime of identity theft, and a complex legal issue arose regarding whether the driver should be responsible for the injuries suffered by the others. In the end, none of them received proper treatment for their injuries and they all left Korea early with their sick bodies, fleeing back to their home country.

While they may have thought it was a wise decision to consider legal expenses, in my opinion, it was a foolish and unwise action. If they left Australia in that state, all responsibility would likely fall on the person who left. They made an emotional decision when comparing the punishment for the crime of identity theft to the amount of compensation they should receive for future medical expenses.

In dealing with injuries from car accidents, one should always be careful and consider the long-term effects, such as post-traumatic stress disorder after the accident.

RENT A HOUSE

Upon arrival in Australia, the first thing to take care of is accommodation. Until finding a suitable place to live, backpacker-style short-term accommodation can be an option.

Rental prices across Australia are rapidly increasing, with advertised rental prices rising by 6.7% over the past 12 months according to data from PropTrack.

Rent prices vary greatly depending on location, area, room size, and number of rooms. However, looking at the rental prices for an unfurnished house in major Australian cities as of February 2023, the approximate rental prices are as follows:

Median house rents in March 2023 (Source: PropTrack)

City	Median house rent	Annual change
Sydney	$650	+8.3%
Melbourne	$480	+6.7%
Brisbane	$550	+11.1%
Adelaide	$500	+13.6%
Perth	$520	+13.0%
Hobart	$550	+5.8%
Darwin	$620	+3.3%
ACT	$690	+3.0%
All capital cities	$550	+11.1%

In addition, it is important to consider depositing about two weeks' worth of security deposit upon moving in. In many cases, working holiday makers save on rent by sharing a house with 3-4 people and splitting the rent, or they might choose to live in a share house or board where they rent an empty room from an Australian and possibly share meals together while also learning English.

The cost of lodging or boarding depends on the negotiation with the landlord, and for Australian elderly people who live alone, they often rent out their rooms without making a significant profit, so it may be possible to find a place to stay for around $100 per week.

In reality, finding a short-term rental of an entire house for a working holiday maker who needs to move around to travel and work may not be easy. Even if one is found, the burden of paperwork and deposits required by real estate agents can lead to giving up on renting a house and opting for boarding instead. However, if 2-3 people can rent a house together and share the rental cost, they can have a very flexible and convenient lifestyle, making it worth considering renting a house.

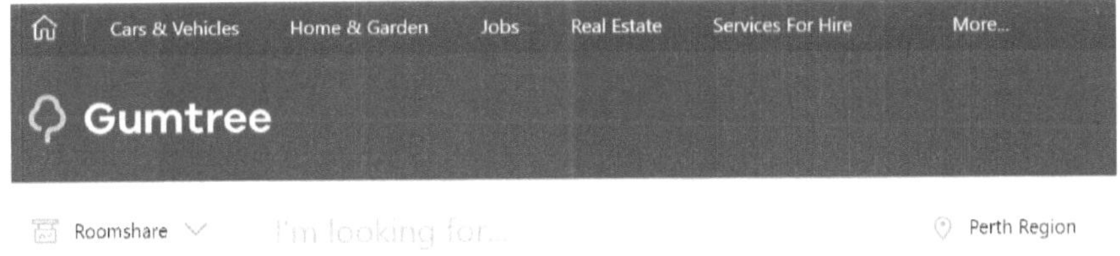

To find a place to live alone, you can usually use advertisements for solo living spaces in most local newspapers. However, if you have access to the internet, you can find many ads for shared living spaces on www.gumtree.com.au .

As shown in the picture above, select [Roomshare] on the left, enter the desired location on the right, and click the magnifying glass icon.

If you can't find a suitable share house on Gumtree, another way to find one is to post an ad looking for a share house. One website for share house ads is called www.flatmates.com.au. This is a very convenient space for both those looking for a room and those offering one, as it is used by both. To register, simply type the address www.flatmates.com.au into Google.

I need a room

Create a listing for people
filling a room to find you.

Find a place

Click on the [Find a place] button on the left side of the main screen. Then, after signing up, enter the type of accommodation you want and your contact information, and wait for a response.

When looking for accommodation in Australia, the following terms are commonly used:

- Room(s) in existing share house - a room in a house that is already shared by others
- Whole property - a standalone property
- Studio flat - a self-contained room
- Granny flat - a small, independent house attached to a main house
- 1 bed flat - a one-bedroom apartment
- Homestay - renting a room in a local family's home and living with them
- Shared room - a room shared with another person
- Student accommodation - dormitory-style accommodation for students.

PREPARING AN ENGLISH RESUME

If you have arrived in Australia, found accommodation, and bought a car, the next step is to find a job. The first thing a job seeker needs to do is to prepare an impressive English resume that introduces yourself.

A quick tip about Australia!

In Australia, all petrol stations are self-service. First, you put in the fuel, then you go to the cashier and tell them your pump number and pay. Some petrol stations may require pre-payment for late-night refueling. In such cases, the pump won't work until you either go to the cashier and specify how much fuel you want or use the pre-payment machine provided on the pump.

An English resume is a tool that promotes oneself and highlights their strengths to ultimately make them stand out to potential employers and increase their chances of being selected. Therefore, if one is truly motivated to find a job, they should not take the preparation of their resume lightly.

The information that must be included in a resume is what employers want to know from their perspective. If you imagine what employers want to know, you should ensure that the following information is included in the resume: 1) when you can start working, 2) how you can meet the employer's requirements or expectations, 3) the fact that your education or qualifications are suitable for the position the employer is looking for, 4) the fact that you have relevant experience and skills for the position, and 5) the fact that you are the most suitable expert for the position.

There is no set format for an English resume. While it's possible to write it in one's own unique style, there are still commonly used resume writing methods in Australia. If you visit https://www.resume-now.com/ , you can find English resume templates. However, here are some items that should generally be included in a resume:

Contact Details

Your contact details should be located at the top of your resume. This should include your name, address, phone number, mobile number, and email address. Your name, phone number, and email address should be included at the top of each page. Avoid using unprofessional email names and use a dignified name instead. Also, avoid using numbers and letters that can be easily confused, such as the number 0 and the letter "o", or the lowercase "l" and uppercase "I".

Personal Details

As Australia is a signatory to international conventions on human rights, it is prohibited from discriminating on the basis of age, gender, religion, disability, etc. Therefore, there is no obligation to provide specific personal information such as age or marital status on your resume. In fact, it is often better not to mention your age if you are considered too young or inexperienced. However, if you think that providing your birthdate would be advantageous, there is no need to conceal it.

Layout

It is better to keep the overall layout of your resume as simple and clear as possible. Use a font size that is easy to read, with Times New Roman or Arial font and 11 or 12 point size being the most commonly used in Australia. There is no need to waste space by creating a table. Focus on organizing your resume around your contact information and work experience.

Headers should be in a slightly bold font, which is easier to read than using bold and underlining together. You can use bullet points, but use a consistent font type. Avoid using various colors and shapes for bullet points that can create confusion.

Key Strengths or Career Summary

Many resumes in Australia start with key strengths or a career summary. If you choose to include this section, focus on highlighting your most important and relevant skills.

For example,
- High level computer skills in using MS-Office - Advanced computer skills in using Microsoft products
- Three years of experience serving customers at convenience

stores and restaurants - Three years of experience in customer service at restaurants and convenience stores

Instead of listing these strengths, you can also start your resume with a career summary. This is a resume writing technique that the author prefers to use, which involves summarizing your entire career in a few sentences to introduce yourself.

Below is an excerpt from the author's old resume, provided as a sample, so you can consider it as a virtual career summary for reference.

Fluently speaking English, being able to make and translate advanced English documents, especially talented in negotiation with overseas companies, I have experienced the information industries for over 10 years and held the ability to practically develop any application software. Moreover, I have various site experiences of information, investigation, and inquiries acquired while serving as a foreign affairs police investigator.

According to job search expert Mr. Napier, some job seekers include phrases like "to utilise my skills in a professional environment for the mutual benefit of myself and employer" in their career summary, which he considers meaningless and unpleasant to read. Therefore, he advises job seekers to avoid using such expressions in their resumes.

JASON LEE

Contact number: 0400-000-0000
Address: 12 Hilton Ct Wilson 6107 WA
Email: myemail@naver.com

About Me	Hi! I'm a friendly, enthusiastic and mature team worker on a working holiday visa from South Korea. I'm flexibly in search of a casual job, open and excited to various job opportunities. My English is not fluent yet but I'm continuously studying to improve.
Key Skills	• Native Korean speaker • Assembling computer • Computer maintenance • Hard-working with a focus to continually learn and improve
Work Experience	Position: Mechanical design Hyosung Heavy Industries, Changwon City, South Gyeongsang Province, Korea Aug 2021 – Nov 2022
Qualifications	• Industrial Engineer Machinery Design • Graphic Technology Qualification Level 1
Education	Computer Science & Graphics Daejeon National University of Science and Technology Sep 2019 High School Examination Mar 2014
Referee	Name: Bruce Yoon Position: Solicitor Relationship: Landlord Contact number: 0411 898 575

Professional History

After writing the career summary, you can now enter the specific details in reverse chronological order.

For each experience, be sure to include the job title, employer, dates, and responsibilities. Below is a simple one-page English resume, so you can refer to it.

Education & Training

Next, you should describe your education and training. List them in chronological order, starting with the highest degree or qualification obtained. Include the name of the institution, dates attended, graduation/completion status, and degree obtained (e.g. diploma, bachelor's degree, etc.). You can also include any industry training or in-house education.

For example:

The Australian National University, 2/2007 - 12/2008, Master of Law (LL.M.)

Memberships and Licences

List any relevant memberships or licenses in your field of expertise, starting with the most important. Here is an example to refer to.

For example:

10/12/1987 Licensing Department in W.A.   Driver's License A
09/08/1990 Australian Computer Society   Student Member

Hobbies and interests

Including this section in a resume is a matter of personal preference among experts. If you want to include this section, you can list it before the referee section. However, according to some experts, if your hobbies or interests are different from those of the assessor, there is a tendency to exclude you from the selection process, so you should make your own judgment.

A quick tip about Australia!

In Australia, it is common practice to emphasize the role of referees, who serve as guarantors of one's identity. As referees are almost always required in resumes, job applications, and rental agreements, it is advisable to find a socially credible person who can vouch for your identity upon arrival in Australia. Examples of such individuals include local church pastors, priests, police officers, professors, and doctors.

Referees

Referees on a resume typically consist of the names and phone numbers of 2-3 individuals who know the candidate well. It's also a good idea to mention "Written references available upon request" at the end. A sample resume that incorporates these guidelines is included at the end of this book for reference.

APPLYING FOR AN AUSTRALIAN TAX FILE NUMBER (TFN)

To work in Australia, one must first have a Tax File Number (TFN). Without this number, employers cannot hire you. Therefore, the TFN is an essential requirement to work in Australia.

Let's find out where and how to apply for a TFN. You can apply for a TFN at https://www.ato.gov.au/iar . Applying for a TFN is free and very simple. However, if you accidentally end up on https://www.au-taxservices.com/apply , which is a private website that charges a fee to apply for a TFN, make sure to use the official Australian Taxation Office website.

Step 1: Identification

First, when you enter https://www.ato.gov.au/iar on the internet, an instruction screen will appear. Click the green [Start] button to get the following screen:

[Passport or travel document number *] - Enter your passport number.
[Passport or travel document country of origin *] - This is a field to select the country that issued your passport.
[Have you ever visited Australia before? *] - Click "Yes" if you have visited Australia before, or "No" if you have not.
Then, continue to enter the required information in the input fields displayed below the screen.

Identification

All fields marked with * are mandatory.

Travel documentation

We will use the information you enter here to:

> check your details with the Department of Home Affairs
> confirm you are eligible for a TFN.

Enter the information **exactly** as it appears on your passport or travel document.

Passport or travel document number *

Passport or travel document country of origin *

Select

Have you ever visited Australia before? *

◯ Yes

◯ No

[Title] - Men should select "Mr", while women should choose "Mrs" or "Miss" depending on their marital status. If you don't want to indicate your marital status, you can select "Ms".

[Family name *] - This is where you enter your last name as it appears on your passport.

[First given name] - Enter your first name exactly as it appears on your passport. Many Koreans tend to ignore the spaces in their names when typing, but it's important to enter your name exactly as it appears on your passport, including any spaces. For example, a name can be written as Soo Yong or Sooyong. However, legally these are considered different names depending on whether there is a space in the middle, so it's important to enter your name exactly as it appears on your passport.

[Other given names] - This may not apply to most Koreans, so it can be ignored, but if your name is particularly long, you can enter any additional names here.

[Are you, or have you been, known by any other names? *] - If you've ever changed your name, even once, click "Yes" and enter all your previous names here. If not, click "No".

If you clicked "Yes", refer to the following instructions. If you clicked "No", you can skip this and move on to the Tax file number section below.

[Other name type *] - There are many options to choose from here, and each has a different meaning:

Maiden name: This is the name a woman had before she got married.
Name at birth: This is the name you were given at birth.
Assumed name (known as): This is a name you are commonly known by, such as a nickname.
Indigenous name: This is a name used by Indigenous people only.
Previous married name: This is a name you acquired from a previous marriage.
Shortened Name: Nickname
Anglicised Name: Name spelled or modified to conform to English language norms
Other Name: Any other name not covered by the above options.

[Date of Birth *]- Enter the date of birth in the order of day/month/year.

[Gender *]- Choose according to your gender. In the past, many Korean official forms used the term [Sex] in the gender field. A country bumpkin who didn't know what to fill in once wrote "once a week" as his sexual frequency here, holding his belly.

[Do you have a spouse? *]- If you have a spouse, select "Yes", otherwise select "No". For working holiday visa holders who cannot bring family members with them, most are assumed to be unmarried. However, if you got married early and left your spouse in Korea or came to Australia with your spouse for working holiday, you must disclose your spouse's information here.

Step 2: Tax file number

Once you have completed the Identification screen in Step 1, click the green [Next] button at the bottom to move on to Step 2.

[Have you ever applied for a Tax File Number (TFN) or Australian Business Number (ABN) before? *] - This asks if you have previously applied for a TFN or ABN, so answer accordingly.
[Have you ever had a TFN or ABN in your name before? *] - This asks if you have previously had a TFN or ABN in your name. Most likely, the answer will be "No."
[Have you ever lodged a tax return in Australia? *] - This asks if you have previously filed a tax return in Australia. Essentially, it is asking if you have previously applied for a tax refund, which requires a TFN or ABN.
[Do you own property or have other business interest in Australia? *] - This asks if you have any personal property or business interests in Australia.
[I have authorized Centrelink to receive my TFN from the ATO *] - This asks if you have given permission for Centrelink, Australia's comprehensive welfare center, to receive your TFN directly from the Australian Taxation Office.

After entering the information as described above, click the green button [Next] on the bottom right of the screen to proceed to the next step, which is the Address screen.

Step 3: Address

This is where you enter the address where you will receive your TFN via post within 28 days after application. You can use a friend's or relative's address to ensure that you receive it. As you enter the address, the complete address will be automatically generated, so you only need to enter some parts of the address and select the correct option. You can enter the detailed address later. If you need to provide your

Address

All fields marked with * are mandatory.

Australian postal address

Your TFN notice will be posted from the ATO to this address in the next 28 days.

Search address *

Save

Back Cancel

Next

TFN to your employer immediately after applying, you can provide the temporary TFN issued immediately after the online application.

After entering the postal address and clicking [Next], the screen below appears to enter the residential address. If you don't have a permanent address in Australia, you can use an address in your home country.

Current home address

Your residential address cannot be a post office (PO) box number. If you are applying as a temporary visitor you can use your home country address as your residential address.

☐ My residential address is the same as my Australian postal address

Country *

AUSTRALIA

Search address *

e.g. level 15 100 Miller St North Sydney

If the residential address is the same as the postal address where you will receive the TFN, you can tick .

Step 4: Contact

After completing the address input as above, the last step is to enter your contact information. Here, you only need to enter your Australian mobile phone number and email address.

Contact

All fields marked with * are mandatory

You must provide details of at least one person we can contact if we need more information. You may provide contact details for another person if you do not want us to contact you because of your language difficulties, age or illness.

Australian contact details

Your details

Mobile

Phone

Area code   Phone number

Email

☐ I want to provide contact details for another person

If you need to use someone else's contact details because you don't have an Australian contact number, you can enter their mobile phone number and email instead and click on [I want to provide contact details for another person] below.

Then, when the final screen appears as shown below, click on the "Tick this box to sign this declaration" box, confirm that you are not a robot, and click the [Submit] button to finish.

Chapter 5. Is Earning 100 Thousand Dollars within a year Possible?

QUALIFICATIONS FOR EMPLOYMENT

Having a qualification recognized in Australia can definitely be an advantage for employment compared to not having one. However, specialized qualifications often take several years and can be quite costly, which can be impractical. In such cases, if you have a qualification from your home country, you may be able to have it recognized as an equivalent qualification through a skills assessment process in Australia, or you may be able to obtain the qualification in a short period of time by receiving education at a vocational school in Australia by having your work experience recognized in your home country.

Recognition of Prior Learning (RPL)

One such process is the Recognition of Prior Learning (RPL) system, which evaluates the competencies acquired through formal and informal learning to determine if they meet the requirements of the learning unit.

The documents required for RPL application are as follows:

- Records of completed education
- Assessment items
- Assessment records
- Employment verification letter

The RPL evaluation agency in Australia is managed by each state's education department, so it would be best to inquire with the education department of the state in which one resides.

RSA - Responsible Service of Alcohol

In Australia, the RSA certification is required for anyone working in a venue that serves alcohol. With this certification, job seekers can have an advantage when applying for various positions such as bartenders, wait staff, or karaoke hostesses. Obtaining the RSA certification is relatively easy as it can be obtained through an online course for a small fee. As long as you can read and understand English sentences, anyone can obtain the certification within a short period of time.

If you search for RSA online, you can find advertisements that offer the certification for $17.50. By obtaining the RSA certification through an online course, you can significantly increase your job opportunities in Australia.

GETTING A JOB

If you have secured accommodation, have a car and a mobile phone, and have prepared your resume, you can now actively start looking for a job.

Job searching in Australia is primarily done through the following channels:

- Job hunting through personal contacts and newspaper ads
- Utilizing the Working Holiday Program
- Online job search activities
- Seeking job opportunities through recruitment agencies

Job hunting through personal contacts and newspaper ads

For working holidaymakers, it is common to first look for job opportunities through friends or acquaintances, and if their English proficiency is not sufficient, they often end up working for low wages at businesses run by a same ethnic migrant.

However, in my opinion, those with a vocabulary level equivalent to that of a high school graduate in Korea should not be afraid to directly engage in job search activities.

First, I recommend collecting all local newspapers, whether free or paid, and reviewing the job-related sections. If you find a job in your area of interest, don't hesitate to call the phone number listed. Then, you can say something like this:

"I saw your advertisement looking for a cleaner. Is the position still available?"

If the other party says "Yes" or "No", and if you hear something like "No, I'm sorry it is not", you can say "Ok, thank you anyway" and hang up. If you hear "Yes", you can say "I would like to take the job. May I see you as soon as possible?" and arrange to meet them. Then, while stumbling along on the job site, you can learn and get better with each step. The English vocabulary used in this job search is very limited, so after a few tries, the words you use will become clear, and you will gain confidence.

A few years ago, my wife's niece received a working holiday visa to Australia. With the guidance of my daughter, she sent her resume randomly to places with job postings in newspapers. One day, she received a call from a doughnut shop, but feeling unsure of her English skills, she asked my daughter to answer the phone for her. My daughter explained that her cousin wanted to apply for a job at the doughnut shop, but the shop requested to speak with the niece for an interview over the phone. Unfortunately, during the interview, the niece struggled to understand the questions and just kept saying "Yes" without comprehending them. Sensing that something was amiss, I stepped in and explained that my niece had not been in Australia for very long and was still uncomfortable speaking English on the phone. I suggested meeting in person for better understanding.

That's absolutely true. For someone who is not comfortable with English conversation, it's much easier to understand when speaking face-to-face rather than on the phone without being able to see the other person's face. Eventually, we were able to arrange an interview with the doughnut shop owner and a few days later, my niece had an actual interview at the shop. After the interview, she was offered a job and agreed to work there for an hourly wage.

Using Programs Designed for Working Holiday Visa Holders

While searching for job opportunities through newspaper ads is an option, as a holder of a Working Holiday visa, you could consider utilizing programs specifically designed for Working Holidaymakers.

There are companies, such as The Global Work & Travel Co. and Alliance Abroad, that provide tailored programs for Working Holidaymakers, including guaranteed job opportunities during their stay, airport pickup, local settlement introductions, social activities, and more. They can also assist with finding accommodation upon request, as well as help with opening a bank account and applying for a tax identification number.

The following are the website addresses of these companies, so those who are interested can contact them directly:

A. The Global Work & Travel Co.
https://www.globalworkandtravel.com/

B. Alliance Abroad
https://allianceabroad.com/programs/australia/

Online Job Search

It's now become common for many job seekers and employers to use the internet for job searches. In Australia, there are various online platforms that connect job seekers with employers, such as Seek, Indeed, Jora, Career One, and Backpacker Job Board. These platforms make it convenient to find job opportunities that match your needs, and you can easily browse and apply for jobs that fit your situation.

If you're a Working Holidaymaker, it's advisable to narrow your search to short-term or contract positions, which are more suitable for your visa restrictions. Some job ads specifically target Working Holidaymakers, so keep an eye out for those as well. Below are the online addresses of these platforms.

A. Seek
https://www.seek.com.au/

B. Indeed
https://au.indeed.com/

C. Jora
https://au.jora.com/

D. Career One
https://www.careerone.com.au/

E. Backpacker Job Board
https://www.backpackerjobboard.com.au/

Job search through recruitment agencies

When it comes to job searching, using a recruitment agency can be more convenient than trying to find a job on your own. Recruitment agencies search for job opportunities that match a job seeker's skills and experience and assist them throughout the entire hiring process. However, some may hesitate to use a recruitment agency out of concern that they may charge high fees. It's worth noting that in Australia, it's against the law for recruitment agencies to charge job seekers a fee, and they can only charge fees to employers. Some recruitment agencies even directly hire job seekers and send them to work for the employer in need. Ultimately, whether to use a recruitment agency or not is a personal decision that requires careful consideration.

If you choose a recruitment agency, there may be several interviews before the final hiring decision is made. At this time, the agency can provide advice on how to answer interview questions, making it more reassuring than job searching alone. Below are some platforms that provide recruitment services in Australia.

A. Randstad
https://www.randstad.com.au/

B. Edge Employment Solutions
https://www.edge.org.au/

C. Jobrapido
https://au.jobrapido.com/

D. Adecco
https://www.adecco.com.au/

E. 11 Recruitment
https://11recruitment.com.au/

F. Global Work and Travel
https://www.globalworkandtravel.com/

THE AVERAGE WAGE IN AUSTRALIA

After arriving in Australia, it's not uncommon for people to accept a job recommended by a familiar face without fully understanding the wage system in Australia. Sometimes, they may find themselves receiving a wage that is significantly lower than the average hourly rate in Australia, causing dissatisfaction. Therefore, having a basic understanding of Australia's average wage system can be helpful.

According to the Australian Bureau of Statistics, as of November 2022, the average weekly wage for an adult in Australia was calculated to be $1,805.90. This amounts to an annual salary of $93,906.8, which is a 3.2% increase from the previous year.

Average weekly earnings, key statistics

		Nov 2022	Nov 2021 to Nov 2022
		$	% change
	Full-time adult average weekly ordinary time earnings	1,805.90	3.2
Trend	Full-time adult average weekly total earnings	1,875.20	3.4
	All employees average weekly total earnings	1,376.60	3.7
	Full-time adult average weekly ordinary time earnings (a)	1,807.70	3.4
Seasonally Adjusted	Full-time adult average weekly total earnings	1,876.80	3.6
	All employees average weekly total earnings (a)	1,378.60	3.7
	Full-time adult average weekly ordinary time earnings	1,807.70	3.4
Original	Full-time adult average weekly total earnings	1,878.50	3.6
	All employees average weekly total earnings	1,378.60	3.7

(a) This component is not seasonally adjusted.

Since July 1st, 2022, the Australian statutory minimum wage is $21.38, which corresponds to a weekly wage of $812.60 for a 38-hour workweek.

Therefore, if you come to work in Australia, you should be paid at least this amount. Additionally, if you are not in a permanent position, you should receive a 25% increase on this rate. In other words, while the minimum wage is $21.38 for permanent employees, you should be paid $26.73 per hour as a non-permanent employee.

Sometimes, when you apply for a job, the employer may require a training period to assess your ability to perform the job. During this period, which may last 1-2 weeks, some employers refer to it as a "trial" or "probation" period and may not pay you a salary. However, in Australia, employers are strictly regulated when it comes to unpaid work.

Usually, to evaluate whether a candidate has the necessary skills to perform the job, a supervisor would accompany the candidate during the training period. If the employer requires you to work without pay for a certain period, just to assess your ability, it is considered illegal unpaid work.

The rights of Australian workers are detailed on the Fair Work Ombudsman website (https://www.fairwork.gov.au/), and it is recommended to refer to it for more information.

IS IT POSSIBLE TO EARN 100 THOUSAND DOLLARS IN A YEAR?

There is a reason why the title of this book is "Australian Working Holiday Maker for 1 million dollars." Even though you might wonder how someone without any skills or knowledge can make money as a working holiday maker in Australia, the author shares the real-life experiences of working holiday makers that he witnessed.

To earn one million dollars in a year, an individual must earn approximately $8,400 per month, which equates to a weekly income of around $1,940. For those who have specialized skills such as programming or pipe welding, earning over $2,000 per week is a relatively easy task. Welders who specialize in welding special pipes can earn between $60 to $120 per hour when they go out to a job site. Even if they earn a minimum wage of $60 per hour based on a 38-hour work week, their weekly income would still be $2,280.

However, for most young working holiday makers, earning $2,000 per week is challenging, and they must earn at least $52.60 per hour based on a 38-hour work week. For those who lack specialized skills, finding a job that pays such a high wage can be difficult, except for in cases where they work in dangerous mining or construction sites with special circumstances.

Despite this, a young man from Korea shared with me his story of challenging himself to earn 1 million dollars. In 2018, at the age of 28, he obtained a working holiday visa to come to Western Australia. At that time, the minimum wage in Australia was $18.93 per hour. After living in the Perth area for a short while, he heard rumors that the cost of living in a more remote rural area could be better, and so he flew to a small city located at the northern end of Western Australia. To the best of my recollection, it was Kununurra, which is close to the Northern Territory border.

This place had a shortage of available workforce, so most of the major jobs in the town, such as those at the shopping center, were taken by Korean working holiday makers. Fortunately, the first job this person found was a night security job that came with free accommodation. They worked 8-hour shifts from 10 pm to 6 am, and would usually wake up around 10 or 11 am when they got back to the accommodation. In order to earn more money during the day, they looked for other job opportunities and ended up working an 8-hour shift at a convenience store from 10 am to 6 pm.

By doing this, he was able to earn around $1,800 per week, an amount that was unimaginable in Korea at the time, he said.

When the author met this young man at the end of 2018, he boasted of having found another job. He said he earned an additional $300 per week by doing cleaning work on weekends, bringing his weekly total to $2,100. When asked if he found it exhausting, he replied that he didn't need much sleep and that making money instead of just having fun had become his hobby since he had come to Australia to earn money.

The young man's words were not false. While not everyone can earn 100 thousand dollars, there are opportunities in Australia for those who work hard. However, as in the case of this young man, finding even three jobs is not easy, and it must be done with one's health in mind.

To conclude the title of this book, it means that although it is very difficult for a working holiday maker in Australia to earn over 100 thousand dollars, in a short time of one year, it is not entirely impossible. If you want to take up the challenge, here are some things to keep in mind.

1.   **Choose a high-paying job.** Easy and common jobs that many Korean working holidaymakers do in Australia pay low wages. IT, medical, engineering, and finance industries are some of the high-paying sectors in Australia. Jobs in these industries pay much higher wages than those in the service and consumer industries.

2.   **Work hard, like the young person mentioned earlier.** If there's an opportunity for overtime, take it first, and working on weekends or at night can earn you more income. If your health allows it, finding additional work to earn extra income on weekends or in the

evening can also be helpful. Having multiple jobs is very common in Australia.

3. **Negotiate boldly with your employer for a better salary.** Most Koreans are hesitant to make direct demands to their employers, worrying that it may be considered impolite. However, in Australia, seeking reasonable compensation that matches your skills and experience is viewed as a competent action because you need to assert your rights.

4. **Practice saving money.** Making money is important, but it's even more important to use it wisely. So, refrain from wasteful spending. In particular, Korean working holidaymakers should be careful when visiting casinos since they can easily fall into the allure of gambling, something they may not have experienced before in Korea.

5. **Save on taxes.** Keep detailed records, including receipts, for tax refund applications. Australia has a high tax rate, so tax reduction is more critical than earning money. This is especially true for working holidaymakers, whose tax rates are higher than those of residents.

AUSTRALIAN TAXES AND TAX SAVINGS

Prior to January 1, 2017, working holiday makers were subject to the same tax rate as Australian permanent residents or citizens, in accordance with Australia's residency rules.

However, some working holiday makers took advantage of this regulation by not reporting their income or fleeing back to their home country, or by colluding with some Australian permanent residents or citizens to commit tax evasion.

Therefore, from January 1, 2017, working holiday makers have been subject to a special tax rate with a progressive tax system. As saving on taxes is just as important as earning money in Australia, it is crucial to understand Australia's tax rates and learn how to save on taxes in certain situations.

As of May 10, 2023, the tax rates applicable to working holiday makers are as follows:

Taxable income	Tax rate
0 to $45,000	15%
$45,001 to $120,000	$6,750 plus 32.5% on income over $45,000 up to $120,000
$120,001 to $180,000	$31,125 plus 37% on income over $120,000 up to $180,000
$180,000 and over	$53,325 plus 45% on income over $180,000

The tax regulations for Working Holiday Makers (backpackers) impose higher tax rates than those paid by other Australian residents. This means that, as shown in the table above, working holiday makers are subject to a tax rate of 15% on all income up to $45,000 without any tax-free threshold, and a marginal tax rate ranging from 32.5% to a maximum of 45% on income above that amount.

In 2017, a British woman named Addy who was on a working holiday in Australia for two years applied for a tax refund for her income of $26,576 before returning to the UK. The Australian Taxation Office issued a notice for her to pay 15% tax according to the new tax law effective July 1, 2017. Addy claimed that the tax rate applied to her violated the international agreement between Australia and the UK, and demanded that the Australian Taxation Commissioner apply the same tax rate as for Australian residents. If the same tax rate as for Australian residents was applied, Addy would not have had to pay any tax as her income was less than the then tax-free threshold of $37,000.

The initial ruling of the Australian Federal Court at the time sided with the tax office, stating that "the backpacker tax is consistent with the obligations under the agreement between Australia and the UK." However, Addy appealed this decision, and it was ruled that according to the agreement between Australia and the UK, Addy should be subject to resident tax rates.

Following this ruling, nationals of countries that have signed tax treaties with Australia, including a non-discrimination clause, and who participate in the working holiday visa program, are eligible to be subject to resident tax rates if they meet the residency requirements under the tax law. Currently, the only countries that have signed tax treaties with Australia that include a non-discrimination clause are Chile, Finland, Germany, Israel, Japan, Norway, Turkey, and the UK.

If you want to minimize your tax bill, it's important to keep careful records of your expenses so you can use them when applying for a tax refund. This means keeping track of all the costs you incur in order to earn income. For example, if your work involves cleaning and moving from one location to another, you can claim expenses such as the cost of maintaining your vehicle, fuel, insurance, and parking, as well as any expenses for work clothes or safety gear. For more information on tax minimization strategies, it's a good idea to consult the Australian Taxation Office website (https://www.ato.gov.au/) or seek advice from a qualified expert.

WHAT ARE SOME SUITABLE JOBS FOR WORKING HOLIDAY MAKERS?

There are various job opportunities available for working holiday makers in Australia. Australia offers opportunities to work in different industries and fields, and there are various jobs available for working holiday makers, such as hotels, restaurants, cafes, convenience stores, petrol stations, supermarkets, and more.

Additionally, there are various industries such as construction, agriculture, mining, manufacturing, and more, where working holiday makers can work. There are no restrictions on the types of jobs that working holiday makers can take in Australia, and if one has the skills and abilities, they can work in their desired field. However, to work in Australia, it is essential to have an understanding of the job market, regulations, and lifestyle in Australia.

Bartender - For a sociable working holidaymaker with some proficiency in English, working as a bartender in a bar or restaurant that serves Australia's finest gin, whiskey, and wine is a great option. However, before serving drinks, they must complete RSA (Responsible Service of Alcohol) training to learn about Australia's liquor-related regulations. The advantage of being a bartender is that the hourly wage is high since most work is done in the evenings or on weekends.

Housekeeping - is a very popular job among backpackers and working holidaymakers in Australia since they often provide free accommodation in beautiful and stunning tourist destinations. Ads for housekeepers in hostels, hotels, and boutique homestays should also be considered.

Waiter - Like bartending, waiting tables at an Australian restaurant can be fun and practical for working holidaymakers. If the restaurant has a liquor license, they may also need to provide all RSA certifications. However, waiting tables is ideal for working holidaymakers as it is low-cost and requires no special training.

Fruit Picker - Fruit picking is one of the most popular jobs for working holiday makers on a farm. It's no wonder because the pay is usually high, accommodation is often provided, and it can also count towards eligibility for a second working holiday visa. Specific education or certification is not usually required to work on a farm, but safety equipment such as gloves, safety boots, and work clothes may be necessary. If you plan to work in this field, it's a good idea to prepare your own safety gear that fits you well in Korea before coming to Australia as the price of such equipment may be cheaper in Korea than in Australia.

Receptionist or Administrative Assistant - Women who are proficient in English conversation and have good social skills might want to try these types of jobs. These types of jobs usually have office hours, working Monday to Friday from 9 am to 5 pm, and most receive pay higher than the minimum wage. Most companies require cheerful and friendly people at the counter to satisfy their customers, so there is a high demand for this type of work. If you submit your resume to multiple places and are able to secure an interview, you have a high chance of success if you dress neatly and have a positive attitude.

Construction Worker - Cities and regions in Australia always have construction sites, and due to the government's large-scale construction support in response to the last COVID crisis, the construction industry currently has a high demand but a shortage of workers to complete contracts, making it a difficult field to work in. This means that there are various job opportunities for Korean working holiday makers. In addition, working at a construction site allows one to obtain qualifications for a second working holiday visa.

To work on a construction site, you must have a White Card, which indicates that you are ready to work safely. The White Card course usually takes only a day to complete, and the cost is typically less than AUD $50. The course may also include the cost of equipment such as gloves, safety boots, and safety glasses for an additional fee.

Don't underestimate the job of a construction worker. In Australia, even just managing vehicles on a construction site can earn a daily wage that far exceeds the minimum wage.

Among the industries that many Asians have entered, welding and tile work are common. However, tile work requires crouching and working, which is something that white Australians who are used to a more comfortable lifestyle may not be able to handle. Additionally, a tile worker does not need a certification and it is easy to learn.

Annexure

1. Sample Working Holiday Visa Application

OFFICIAL: Sensitive
Personal Privacy

Australian Government **Department of Home Affairs**	Department of Home Affairs Application for a Working Holiday Visa	**Not Yet Lodged**

Terms and Conditions

View Terms and Conditions   View Privacy statement
Yes
I have read and agree to the terms and conditions

Application context

Current location

Give details of the applicant's current location.
Current location: **KOREA, SOUTH**
Select the applicant's citizenship or visa status in their current location.
Legal status: **Citizen**

Current application

Will the applicant be accompanied by dependent children at any time during their stay in Australia on this visa?
          No

Has the applicant ever been granted and entered Australia on a Work and Holiday visa (subclass 462) before?
          No

COVID-19 affected visa details

Was the last Working Holiday visa held by the applicant a COVID-19 affected visa?
          No

Application Type

Select the type of working holiday visa the applicant is applying for:
          First Working Holiday visa (subclass 417)
Has the applicant been granted and entered Australia on a first Working Holiday visa (subclass 417) before?
          No

Proposed arrival date

Proposed arrival date: **15 Apr 2023**

Application for a Working Holiday Visa

Applicant

Information: Entering names incorrectly may result in denial of permission to board an aircraft to Australia, or result in delays in border processing on arrival to Australia, even if the applicant has been granted a visa.

Passport details

Enter the following details as they appear in the applicant's personal passport.

Family name:	**Lee**
Given names:	**Jinyong**
Sex:	**Male**
Date of birth:	**05 Dec 1997**
Passport number:	**M000X6497**
Country of passport:	**KOREA, REPUBLIC OF (SOUTH) - KOR**
Nationality of passport holder:	**KOREA, REPUBLIC OF (SOUTH) - KOR**
Date of issue:	**24 May 2022**
Date of expiry:	**24 May 2027**
Place of issue / issuing authority:	**Ministry of Foreign Affairs**

It is strongly recommended that the passport be valid for at least six months.

National identity card

Does this applicant have a national identity card?
Yes

National identity card

Enter details exactly as shown on the national identity card.

Family name:	**Lee**
Given names:	**Jinyong**
Identification number:	**971205-1110000**
Country of issue:	**KOREA, SOUTH**

Note: If the National identity card does not have a Date of issue or a Date of expiry, do not enter a date. Leave the field/s blank.

Date of issue:

Date of expiry:

Place of birth

Town / City:	**Dongrae-gu**
State / Province:	**Busan**
Country of birth:	**KOREA (SO STATED)**

Application for a Working Holiday Visa

Relationship status

Relationship status: **Never Married**

Other names / spellings

Is this applicant currently, or have they ever been known by any other names?
Yes

Other names / spellings

Family name: **Lee**
Given names: **Sunyong**
Reason for name change: **Other**
Give details: **To avoid being bullied**

Citizenship

Is this applicant a citizen of the selected country of passport (KOREA, REPUBLIC OF (SOUTH))?
Yes
Is this applicant a citizen of any other country?
No

Other passports or documents for travel

Does this applicant have any other passports or documents for travel?
No

Other identity documents

Does this applicant have other identity documents?
Yes

Other identity documents

Enter details exactly as shown on the identity document.

Family name: **Lee**
Given names: **Jinyong**
Type of document: **Drivers licence**
Identification number: **12-00-620691-00**
Country of issue: **KOREA, SOUTH**

Health examination

Has this applicant undertaken a health examination for an Australian visa in the last 12 months?
No

Application for a Working Holiday Visa

Critical data confirmation

All information provided is important to the processing of this application.
If the information included on this page is incorrect, it may lead to denial of permission to board an aircraft to Australia, even if a visa has been granted.
Confirm that the following information is correct and that it is in the correct fields.

Family name:	**Lee**
Given names:	**Jinyong**
Sex:	**Male**
Date of birth:	**05 Dec 1997**
Country of birth:	**KOREA (SO STATED)**
Passport number:	**M000X6497**
Country of passport:	**KOREA, REPUBLIC OF (SOUTH) - KOR**
Is the above information correct?	**Yes**

Contact details

Country of residence

Usual country of residence: **KOREA, SOUTH**

Department office

The applicant may be required to attend an Australian Government Office for an interview. Which is the closest office to the applicant's current location?

Office: **South Korea, Seoul**

Residential address

Note that a street address is required. A post office address cannot be accepted as a residential address.

Country:	**KOREA, SOUTH**
Address:	**Any APT 501ho,**
	35, Yeogobuk-ro 23beon-gil,
Suburb / Town:	**Dongnae-gu,**
State or Province:	**BUSAN-GWANGYEOSKI (BUSAN)**
Postal code:	**47838**

Postal address

Is the postal address the same as the residential address?

Application for a Working Holiday Visa

Yes

Contact telephone numbers

Enter numbers only with no spaces.
Home phone:
Business phone:
Mobile / Cell phone: **01099009900**

Email address

Email address: **bruce@changalic.com.au**

Authorised recipient

Does the applicant authorise another person to receive written correspondence on their behalf?
This authorises the department to send the authorised person all written correspondence that would
otherwise be sent directly to the applicant.
Yes, a legal practitioner
This person is referred to as the 'authorised recipient'.
Has the applicant appointed this person to provide them immigration assistance?
Yes

Legal practitioner contact details

Legal practitioner

Legal practitioner number **5511104**
(LPN)
Family name: **Yoon**
Given names: **Bruce**
Organisation: **Chan Galic Barristers & Solicitors**

Postal address

Country: **AUSTRALIA**
Address: **50 Melville Parade**
Suburb / Town: **SOUTH PERTH**
State / Territory: **Western Australia**
Postcode: **6151**

Contact telephone numbers

Enter numbers only with no spaces.
Business phone: **0893252611**
Mobile / Cell phone: **0411898575**

Application for a Working Holiday Visa

Electronic communication

The Department prefers to communicate electronically as this provides a faster method of communication.
All correspondence, including notification of the outcome of the application will be sent to:
Email address: **bruce@changalic.com.au**

Note: The holder of this email address may receive a verification email from the Department if the address has not already been verified. If the address holder receives a verification email, they should click on the link to verify their address before this application is submitted.

Occupation and education

Occupation

Usual occupation of the applicant: **Engineer**

Does the applicant intend to work during their time in Australia?
Yes
Select the industry the applicant intends to seek employment in.
Industry type: **Information Media and Telecommunications**

Education

Select the applicant's highest qualification
Qualification: **Graduate Diploma**

Health declarations

In the last five years, has any applicant visited, or lived, outside their country of passport, for more than 3 consecutive months? Do not include time spent in Australia.
No

Does any applicant intend to enter a hospital or a health care facility (including nursing homes) while in Australia?
No

Does any applicant intend to work as, or study or train to be, a health care worker or work within a health care facility while in Australia?
No

Does any applicant intend to work, study or train within aged care or disability care while in Australia?
No

Does any applicant intend to work or be a trainee at a child care centre (including preschools and creches) while in Australia?
No

Application for a Working Holiday Visa

Does any applicant intend to be in a classroom situation for more than 3 months (eg. as either a student, teacher, lecturer or observer)?

No

Has any applicant:
- ever had, or currently have, tuberculosis?
- been in close contact with a family member that has active tuberculosis?
- ever had a chest x-ray which showed an abnormality?

No

During their proposed visit to Australia, does any applicant expect to incur medical costs, or require treatment or medical follow up for:
- blood disorder
- cancer
- heart disease
- hepatitis B or C and/or liver disease
- HIV infection, including AIDS
- kidney disease, including dialysis
- mental illness
- pregnancy
- respiratory disease that has required hospital admission or oxygen therapy
- other?

No

Does any applicant require assistance with mobility or care due to a medical condition?

No

Character declarations

If the applicant answers 'Yes' to any of the character declarations they must give all relevant details. For combined applications, state which applicant the declaration applies to.
If the matter relates to a criminal conviction, provide:
- the date and nature of the offence
- full details of the sentence
- dates of any period of imprisonment or other detention.

Has any applicant ever been charged with any offence that is currently awaiting legal action?

No

Has any applicant ever been convicted of an offence in any country (including any conviction which is now removed from official records)?

No

Has any applicant ever been the subject of a domestic violence or family violence order, or any other order, of a tribunal or court or other similar authority, for the personal protection of another person?

No

Has any applicant ever been the subject of an arrest warrant or Interpol notice?

No

Has any applicant ever been found guilty of a sexually based offence involving a child (including where no conviction was recorded)?

No

Has any applicant ever been named on a sex offender register?

No

Has any applicant ever been acquitted of any offence on the grounds of unsoundness of mind or insanity?

No

Has any applicant ever been found by a court not fit to plead?

No

Has any applicant ever been directly or indirectly involved in, or associated with, activities which would represent a risk to national security in Australia or any other country?

No

Has any applicant ever been charged with, or indicted for: genocide, war crimes, crimes against humanity, torture, slavery, or any other crime that is otherwise of a serious international concern?

No

Has any applicant ever been associated with a person, group or organisation that has been or is involved in criminal conduct?

No

Has any applicant ever been associated with an organisation engaged in violence or engaged in acts of violence (including war, insurgency, freedom fighting, terrorism, protest) either overseas or in Australia?

No

Has any applicant ever served in a military force, police force, state sponsored / private militia or intelligence agency (including secret police)?

No

Has any applicant ever undergone any military/paramilitary training, been trained in weapons/ explosives or in the manufacture of chemical/biological products?

No

Has any applicant ever been involved in people smuggling or people trafficking offences?

No

Has any applicant ever been removed, deported or excluded from any country (including Australia)?

No

Has any applicant ever overstayed a visa in any country (including Australia)?

No

Has any applicant ever had any outstanding debts to the Australian Government or any public authority in Australia?

No

Working holiday declarations

Warning:
Giving false or misleading information is a serious offence.
The applicant declares that they:

Application for a Working Holiday Visa

Understand that they must abide by the conditions of the visa.

Yes

Understand that the visa they are applying for does not permit them to be employed in Australia with one employer for more than 6 months without prior permission.

Yes

Understand that the visa they are applying for does not permit them to undertake studies or training for more than 4 months.

Yes

Have sufficient funds for the initial period of their stay in Australia and for the fare to their intended overseas destination on leaving Australia.

Yes

Understand that any employment is incidental to their holiday in Australia and the purpose of working is to supplement their holiday funds.

Yes

Declarations

Warning:

Giving false or misleading information is a serious offence.

The applicants declare that they:

Have read and understood the information provided to them in this application.

Yes

Have provided complete and correct information in every detail on this form, and on any attachments to it.

Yes

Understand that if any fraudulent documents or false or misleading information has been provided with this application, or if any of the applicants fail to satisfy the Minister of their identity, the application may be refused and the applicant(s), and any member of their family unit, may become unable to be granted a visa for a specified period of time.

Yes

Understand that if documents are found to be fraudulent or information to be incorrect after the grant of a visa, the visa may subsequently be cancelled.

Yes

Understand that if this application is approved, any person not included in this application will not have automatic right of entry to Australia.

Yes

Will inform the Department in writing immediately as they become aware of a change in circumstances (including change of address) or if there is any change relating to information they have provided in or with this application, while it is being considered.

Yes

Have read the information contained in the Privacy Notice(Form 1442i).

Yes

Application for a Working Holiday Visa

Understand that the department may collect, use and disclose the applicant's personal information (including biometric information and other sensitive information) as outlined in the Privacy Notice(Form 1442i).

Yes

Give consent to the collection of their fingerprints and facial image if required.

Yes

Understand that, if required to provide their fingerprints and facial image, the applicant's fingerprints and facial image and biographical information held by the Department may be given to Australian law enforcement agencies to help identify the applicant and determine eligibility for grant of the visa being applied for, and for law enforcement purposes.

Yes

Give consent to Australian law enforcement agencies disclosing the applicant's biometric, biographical and criminal record information to the Department to help identify the applicant, to determine eligibility for grant of a visa and for law enforcement purposes.

Yes

Give consent to the Department using the applicant's biometric, biographical and criminal record information obtained for the purposes of the Migration Act 1958 or the Citizenship Act 2007.

Yes

As an applicant:

I understand that if my visa ceases to be in effect and I do not hold another visa to remain in Australia at that time, I will be an unlawful non-citizen under the Migration Act 1958. As such, I will be expected to depart from Australia, and be subject to removal under the Migration Act 1958.

Yes

Australian values

Each applicant who is 18 years or over has read, or had explained to them, information provided by the Australian Government on Australian society and values, and agrees to the Australian values statement.

Yes

Life in Australia booklet   Australian values statement

2. Letter to Car Dealer

Your name
Your address
Your phone number
Your email address (if you have one)

Date

Name of dealer
Street
Suburb/Town
State Postcode

Dear Sir/Madam

Re: (insert vehicle make, model and registration number)

On (date) I purchased a motor vehicle from your dealership (put the vehicle details here, for example, year, make, model and registration number). Unfortunately, the vehicle has not been satisfactory because (say what the problem is, for example, it is leaking oil from the engine. If you have already taken the car back, state what action has been taken and what the results have been, for example, 'Your mechanic inspected my vehicle and agreed to fix the problem under warranty, however, when I collected the vehicle and started using it again, the problem was still there').

I would appreciate it if you could organise to (say what you want the dealer to do, for example, have the problem fixed/use another repairer to fix the problem) by (date). As I am sure you can appreciate, I rely on my car for transport and apart from the inconvenience, this problem has also caused me to incur additional cost (I have kept the receipts as proof).

I look forward to settling this matter amicably. If, however, the matter is not satisfactorily resolved by (date), I will consider taking further action to resolve the complaint either through the Department of Commerce or through the courts.

Yours faithfully

(Your signature)
(Your name)

3. Sample Resume

JOE SMITH

---

205 Smith Drive, Smithville NSW 2008
Home ph: 02 9000 5555   Mobile: 0444 444 444   Email: e.smith@hotmail.com

CAREER OVERVIEW

A sales management professional with seven years' experience in the media industry, I have worked on newspaper, web and television products. I have a proven track record of developing new business and motivating a team to consistently exceed targets. I've recently completed a Masters of Business Administration and am now seeking a new professional challenge.

KEY STRENGTHS

The aim of the section is to give the person reading your resume a quick snapshot of what you have to offer in the hope they instantly place you in the short list pile. As a guide, six points is good but there is no real rule. Another tip, be specific. I see a lot of "Excellent Communication Skills" but what does that mean? Here are some examples:

- High level computer skills including Excel, Word and Powerpoint
- Five years experience in customer service both face to face and phone based
- Strong business development capabilities with European experience
- Experience developing sales and marketing collateral
- Active toastmasters public speaker

CAREER HISTORY

May 2003 – Present Sales Manager

Global Web Media

Describe the company's main activity or focus. This is appropriate for those coming from overseas or in cases where the company might be largely unknown. Organisations like IBM, News Limited, Suncorp or the big banks, to name a few examples, will need no explanation.

Key responsibilities

Provide detailed summary of the role's key responsibilities and accountabilities. Do not go for the longest list, be concise and to the point. Try not to include the obvious i.e. – to meet sales targets.

Sourced from http://career-advice.careerone.com.au/resume-cover-letter/sample-resume/sample-resume-kate-southam-recommended/article.aspx

- Develop and execute sales strategies
- Maintain and strengthen a large portfolio of clients
- Coach, mentor and motivate sales team
- Manage sales budgets and set targets

Key achievements

- Closed major deals and followed up senior business relationships with Universal McCann, Columbia Pictures, Starcom and Viacom
- Named employee of the Year 2004

Feb 2001- Apr 2003 Business Development Executive

D&D Media, London

Company description

Key responsibilities

- Develop relationships across targeted accounts
- Manage all sales related aspects for allocated accounts
- Review pricing and service levels
- Identify new sales and marketing opportunities
- Develop product literature and sales collateral

Key achievements

- X
- X
- X

EDUCATION & TRAINING

Start with your highest qualification first

- 1996 - 1999 University of Sydney

Bachelor of Commerce – majoring in Marketing & International Business

- 1998 Saint Louis University, Madrid, Spain

Semester exchange program

- 1989 - 1995 Sydney Boys High School

Higher School Certificate, UAI 95.8

Sourced from http://career-advice.careerone.com.au/resume-cover-letter/sample-resume/sample-resume-kate-southam-recommended/article.aspx

- o   July 2005 Negotiation skills course

Eastern Suburbs Community College

- o   Oct 2004 Internal workshop - Building customer relationships

Global Web Media

- o   Aug 2003 Sales Management Training

XYZ Sales Training College

PROFESSIONAL MEMBERSHIPS

Include only those relevant to your career. Some examples:

- o   Media Industry Association: Member since: May 2001
- o   Newspaper Association of Australia: Member since: 2002

HOBBIES & INTERESTS

- o   Waterskiing
- o   Rock climbing
- o   Cooking
- o   Travel

REFEREES

Some people choose to include their referees while others do not.

Option 1:

Referees will be provided upon request

Option 2:

Name: [insert name]

Company: [insert company name, location]

Relationship: [Provide details of professional relationship e.g. former manager at company XYZ]

Email: [insert email address]

Land Line: [insert land line contact details]

Mobile: [insert mobile contact details]

Australian Working Holiday Maker for 1 million dollars

Australian Working Holiday Maker for 1 million dollars

ABOUT THE AUTHOR

The author of this book, Lawyer Bruce Yoon, previously worked as a foreign affairs detective for five years before leaving for Australia to study computer science. After working in software development and consulting, he pursued theological studies while participating in M&A projects. Later, while running IT/BT businesses, he enrolled in law school and became a lawyer.

In addition to this book, the author has written various books on different topics, such as "My Experiences in Korea and Australia," "Korean Trailblazers," " The Story of a Korean Police Officer who became an Australian Lawyer ", "South Korea After 30 Years - The Future of South Korea Predicted by AI ChatGPT," and "Comparative Essays on Australian and Korean Law and Culture."